797,885 Books
are available to read at

Forgotten Books

www.ForgottenBooks.com

Forgotten Books' App
Available for mobile, tablet & eReader

ISBN 978-1-331-62657-2
PIBN 10214791

This book is a reproduction of an important historical work. Forgotten Books uses
state-of-the-art technology to digitally reconstruct the work, preserving the original format
whilst repairing imperfections present in the aged copy. In rare cases, an imperfection in
the original, such as a blemish or missing page, may be replicated in our edition. We do,
however, repair the vast majority of imperfections successfully; any imperfections that
remain are intentionally left to preserve the state of such historical works.

Forgotten Books is a registered trademark of FB &c Ltd.
Copyright © 2015 FB &c Ltd.
FB &c Ltd, Dalton House, 60 Windsor Avenue, London, SW19 2RR.
Company number 08720141. Registered in England and Wales.

For support please visit www.forgottenbooks.com

1 MONTH OF FREE READING

at
www.ForgottenBooks.com

By purchasing this book you are eligible for one month membership to ForgottenBooks.com, giving you unlimited access to our entire collection of over 700,000 titles via our web site and mobile apps.

To claim your free month visit:
www.forgottenbooks.com/free214791

* Offer is valid for 45 days from date of purchase. Terms and conditions apply.

Similar Books Are Available from
www.forgottenbooks.com

Poems
by Edgar Allan Poe

The Complete Poetical Works and Letters of John Keats
by John Keats

Erotica
by Arthur Clark Kennedy

The Complete Poetical Works of John Milton
by John Milton

One Hundred Poems of Kabir
by Kabir

The Barons' Wars, Nymphidia, and Other Poems
by Michael Drayton

A Book of English Poetry
by George Beaumont

Poems: Sonnets, Lyrics, and Miscellaneous
by Edward Blackadder

The Book of Fairy Poetry
by Dora Owen

Chinese Poems
by Charles Budd

Coleridge's The Rime of the Ancient Mariner
And Other Poems, by Samuel Taylor Coleridge

Complaints; Containing Sundrie Small Poemes of the Worlds Vanitie
Whereof the Next Page Maketh Mention, by Edmund Spenser

The Complete Poetical Works of Geoffrey Chaucer
Now First Put Into Modern English, by John S. P. Tatlock

Cursor Mundi (The Cursor of the World)
A Northumbrian Poem of the XIVth Century, by Richard Morris

The Defence of the Bride Other Poems
by Anna Katharine Green

The Divine Comedy, Vol. 1
by Dante Alighieri

The Duke of Gandia
by Algernon Charles Swinburne

Eanthe
A Tale of the Druids, and Other Poems, by Sandford Earle

The Earthly Paradise
A Poem, by William Morris

The English Poems of George Herbert
Newly Arranged in Relation to His Life, by George Herbert Palmer

SELECTED READINGS

LANE

Educ T 759.11.30

F65.5684
8th grade

LIBRARY OF THE

DEPARTMENT OF EDUCATION

COLLECTION OF TEXT-BOOKS
CONTRIBUTED BY THE PUBLISHERS

TRANSFERRED
TO
HARVARD COLLEGE
LIBRARY

3 2044 097 069 405

SELECTED READINGS

FOR
THE EIGHTH GRADE

WITH INTRODUCTION AND NOTES

BY

M. A. L. LANE

GINN AND COMPANY

BOSTON · NEW YORK · CHICAGO · LONDON

COPYRIGHT, 1911, BY
GINN AND COMPANY

ALL RIGHTS RESERVED

911.4

The Athenæum Press
GINN AND COMPANY · PRO-
PRIETORS · BOSTON · U.S.A.

PREFACE

THIS collection of prose and verse "for appreciative reading" in the eighth grade of grammar schools has been made in accordance with the definite requirements of the New York Commissioners of Education, as set forth in the Course of Study and Syllabus for Elementary Schools, published by the University of the State of New York.

In preparing notes for these selections, the editor's purpose has been to supply information, not always easily accessible, which a young reader can hardly be assumed to possess. Words that may be found in all dictionaries, and geographical references which ought to be plain to him, are not included. Much of the benefit as well as the pleasure in reading is lost if all the details of an allusion are made clear, and if nothing is left to the student's own intelligence. On the other hand, his time may be unprofitably spent in pursuing some trivial fact or some bit of unusual knowledge. Special points of interest, such as may belong to the history of a word, or of a certain period, have also been suggested in the notes, but as a rule the annotation has been strictly limited to what is essential to the proper interpretation of the text.

Various editions have been consulted, and the most trustworthy of these have been followed. The introductory notes have been made as brief as possible, being designed merely to give such information as will increase the pupils' appreciation of the selection. The biographical sketches deal with matters likely to be of interest to young readers, rather than with the bare record of events in each author's life. A pronouncing vocabulary of proper names will, it is hoped, save some time and trouble.

CONTENTS

		PAGE
Introduction		vii
The Man without a Country	*Edward Everett Hale*	1
The Skeleton in Armor	*Henry Wadsworth Longfellow*	30
Horatius	*Thomas Babington Macaulay*	35
The Singing Leaves	*James Russell Lowell*	57
Rhœcus	*James Russell Lowell*	60
Washington	*James Russell Lowell*	65
From " Under the Old Elm "		
Incident of the French Camp	*Robert Browning*	66
Under the Willows [Prelude]	*James Russell Lowell*	68
Apostrophe to the Ocean	*Lord Byron*	70
To a Skylark	*Percy Bysshe Shelley*	72
Notes		77
Pronouncing Vocabulary		85

INTRODUCTION

EDWARD EVERETT HALE, one of the great national figures of his time, was born in Boston, Massachusetts, in 1822. He was great as a writer, as an orator, as a preacher, and as a philanthropist. After his graduation from Harvard College at the age of seventeen, he took up journalism and in 1840 was a correspondent at Washington. Needing a wider field for his activity, he became the minister of a parish in Worcester in 1846. As long as he lived he was a preacher, but, as was happily said of him, "he cared more for the Kingdom of God than for any church, local or universal."

In 1848 he became known as a writer, and from that time on his easy, colloquial style and his frequent contributions to many different periodicals made his work familiar to all classes of readers. It was soon recognized that he was the champion of the downtrodden and oppressed, yet he was equally beloved by the prosperous and well-born. He was, in short, as thorough-going a democrat, in the true sense of the word, as this country has produced. His quick wit, the stores of information which his wide reading had opened to him, and especially his ready sympathy with every form of human endeavor, made him the most interesting of companions. Dr. Hale lived in all sorts of active ways, but his great aim was to serve the men and women around him. His four famous mottoes are the watchword of the Lend a Hand Societies, which try to carry out his ideal: —

> Look up and not down;
> Look forward and not back;
> Look out and not in;
> Lend a hand!

viii   SELECTIONS FOR THE EIGHTH GRADE

As a boy he played on the historic Common of his native city, and he knew by heart all the traditions clustering about it. As a young man he listened to the conversation of Daniel Webster, of his uncle, the great orator, Edward Everett (for whom he was named), and of other makers of history. As an older man he identified himself with national movements and institutions. He was for many years minister of a large Boston church. For the last six years of his life he was chaplain of the United States Senate. He died in 1909.

His writing was always a joy and a recreation to him, and his six rules are the secret of successful composition: (1) Know what you want to say. (2) Say it. (3) Use your own language. (4) Leave out the fine passages. (5) Remember that a short word is better than a long one, and that the fewer words the better. (6) Cut it to pieces. Beyond these simple principles, no man was ever less bound by rules than he.

Personally, Dr. Hale was a tall man, with rugged features and a picturesque growth of hair and beard. His voice was heavy and sonorous, often, in moments of indignant protest against some rank injustice, deepening into a roar. Yet so kindly was the gleam in those keen eyes that no one ever hesitated to approach him for help and counsel, nor did one ever leave him without receiving a word of sympathy and cheer.

Henry Wadsworth Longfellow is undoubtedly the most popular of all American poets, and no one could have worked more honestly and faithfully at his chosen craft than he did. He was born at Portland, Maine, in 1807, and was graduated from Bowdoin College in the same class with Hawthorne in 1825. He had distinguished himself in college as a student of modern languages, and soon after his graduation he was appointed professor of these languages at Bowdoin. Later he accepted a similar appointment at Harvard. He bought the old Craigie House, which had once been Washington's headquarters in Cambridge, and there he spent the rest of his life.

INTRODUCTION ix

Longfellow was greatly beloved not only by his personal friends, but by his neighbors and his students, and by children everywhere. As a poet he is characterized by tenderness and feeling, and by smooth and melodious verse.

Longfellow's fame rests largely upon his "Hiawatha," a story of Indian life which is familiar to all American boys and girls. "Evangeline" is also considered one of his great works. He once said of the latter poem to a friend: "It is easy for you to read because it was so hard for me to write." His translations were written with the same conscientious faithfulness that is shown in his other poems, and are deservedly famous.

The Cambridge school children, wishing to give Mr. Longfellow some token of their love, presented to him an armchair made from the wood of the "spreading chestnut tree" mentioned in "The Village Blacksmith." This he regarded as the most precious of all his treasures and relics. He expressed his thanks in the little poem called "From my Armchair." No child who wished to see this chair was ever turned away from his door.

A few days after Longfellow's seventy-fifth birthday he was taken ill, and he died on March 24, 1882. Emerson, his brother poet, whose mind was sadly clouded by age and feebleness, came to the funeral, and as he looked his last upon the serene face he said, "I have forgotten the gentleman's name, but he had a beautiful soul." No truer word of eulogy could have been spoken.

Thomas Babington Macaulay was born in Leicestershire, England, in 1800, and was graduated from Trinity College, Cambridge, in 1822. In 1830 he entered Parliament and began his political career. Four years later he became a member of the Supreme Council of India, and from that time on kept a keen interest in Indian affairs. His system of education is still in force in that country. In 1857 he was raised to the peerage.

As a child Macaulay was very fond of books. From the time that he was three years old they were his constant companions,

SELECTIONS FOR THE EIGHTH GRADE

and before he was eight he had written a romance and a history. At this period of his life, Scott's poems were his chief delight, and with the whole of "Marmion" at his tongue's end, he began to write verses himself. His memory was always a marvelous one. Apparently he remembered everything that he had read or heard. In his later life he was heard to say that if all copies of "Paradise Lost" and "The Pilgrim's Progress" were destroyed, he could reproduce them both from recollection.

Lord Macaulay's "History of England" was the great work of his life, and he gave up his political ambitions so that he might devote himself to it. His presentation of facts is often warped by his own opinions, but for that very reason his "History" is more entertaining than purely judicial statements. The characters are vigorously drawn, and the story is full of color. Five volumes, dealing with a period of less than twenty years, make up this masterpiece, which was originally planned to cover a century.

His fame as a writer of scholarly essays was early established. He was also well known as a poet. The "Lays of Ancient Rome," a collection of ballads which, in the author's own words, aimed to "transform portions of early Roman history back into the poetry of which they were made," became wonderfully popular with both young and old. A few critics, among whom was Matthew Arnold, found fault with them, but no adverse criticism seems to have lessened the favor in which they are held. It is acknowledged that only Scott has written ballads of similar simplicity and force.

Lord Macaulay was a man of much personal charm, and was in great demand as a guest. His gifts as a story-teller, his instant perception of another's meaning, and his swift thought, which was "like lightning," made him welcome wherever he went. He was never married, but his devotion to his sister and to her children was delightful to see. He died at his home in London in 1859, and was buried at Westminster Abbey in the "Poets' Corner."

INTRODUCTION

James Russell Lowell, one of the most scholarly of American poets, was born in Cambridge, Massachusetts, in 1819. He was graduated from Harvard in 1838, and only three years later his first volume of poems was published. Before ten years had gone by he had written "The Vision of Sir Launfal," and the humorous sketch "A Fable for Critics," in which he hits off the weaknesses of the writers of the time. Of himself he says:

> "There is Lowell, who's striving Parnassus to climb
> With a whole bale of *isms* tied together with rhyme;
> He might get on alone, spite of brambles and boulders,
> But he can't with that bundle he has on his shoulders;
> The top of the hill he will ne'er come nigh reaching,
> Till he learns the distinction 'twixt singing and preaching."

Though there was some truth in this one-sided criticism, many of Lowell's fellow countrymen were grateful to him for expressing in the "Biglow Papers" his indignation at the political selfishness which had brought about the Mexican War. To them the mixture of singing and preaching seemed a very effective one.

Lowell succeeded Longfellow in the professorship of modern languages at Harvard, and in 1857, when the *Atlantic Monthly* was established, he became its editor. He was also an editor of the *North American Review*, and many of his poems and essays were first printed in these magazines. As he grew older his poetry, always marked by tender sentiment, sounded deeper notes of patriotism and lofty aspiration.

In 1877 he was sent as Minister Plenipotentiary to Spain, and three years later was transferred to England. He returned to the United States in 1885, and passed the rest of his life in his quiet Cambridge home. Here, in the house where he was born, he died in 1891.

One of the greatest names in English literature is that of Robert Browning. He was born in a suburb of London in 1812, and his boyhood was spent within easy reach of country

xii SELECTIONS FOR THE EIGHTH GRADE

pleasures. He had a garden of his own and kept pets of various kinds. In his poems may be found many proofs of his close acquaintance with country sights and sounds.

Browning's father was a great lover of books, and one of the boy's earliest memories was of sitting on his father's knees before the library fire, and listening to the story of the fall of Troy. When he was still very young he would compose rhymes for his own amusement, and marching round and round the dining table would recite them, marking off the measures with great emphasis. His father had taught him to read by rhyming words, and helped him to learn the Latin declensions in the same way. When at the age of eighteen he entered London University, he had amassed a large quantity of his own writings, but he was still undecided whether he would be a poet, a painter, or a musician. It was not until he was twenty-two years old that "Paracelsus," the first of his poems to appear over his own name, was published. A little later he made his first visit to Italy. Long afterwards, when he was asked whether he had studied at Cambridge or at Oxford, he was wont to say, "Italy is my university."

Italy, indeed, was his home for many years. It was here that he brought his invalid wife, after his romantic marriage in 1846, and here much of his best work was done. When Mrs. Browning died in 1861, his grief and loneliness drove him back to England for a while, but during the rest of his life he lived alternately in London and in various parts of Italy. He died in Venice in 1889, and was buried in Westminster Abbey, not far from the last resting place of Dickens and Macaulay.

Many of Browning's shorter poems make a special appeal to young readers, because they are so charged with hope and energy. He took life cheerfully, never with sighs and lamentings.

> "I find earth not gray, but rosy,
> Heaven not grim, but fair of hue.
> Do I stoop? I pluck a posy.
> Do I stand and stare? All's blue."

INTRODUCTION xiii

These words, which he makes Shakespeare say in "At the Mermaid," are what he could have said himself with as great truth. He is preëminently the poet of steadfastness and unconquerable courage and high endeavor.

Many persons complain that Browning is hard to understand, and it is true that he often requires of his readers a high degree of intelligence and mental agility. To read his most characteristic poems. is not an easy walk along a smooth road, but a brisk climb, in which one must spring from rock to rock, regardless of the roundabout path. He drops out commonplace words and links of thought as casually as a runner leaps across a brook, ignoring the stepping stones that his followers may need. Yet when one has reached the height to which the poet has led the way, there is the feeling of triumph and satisfaction which always rewards the solving of a puzzle, besides the enjoyment of the wider view.

George Gordon, or Lord Byron, as he is generally called, was born in London in 1788. When he was two years old his mother, whose marriage had been an unhappy one, took her little son to Scotland, and there he had his first schooling. The splendid scenery of the Highlands, which he visited when he was six or seven years old, made a deep impression, even at that early age, on his beauty-loving nature. A few years later he inherited the title and estate of his great-uncle, and soon afterwards he entered an English school. Here he showed the same traits for which he was to be remarkable as a grown man. He had much courage and generosity, and a strong sympathy for any kind of suffering. On the other hand, he was quick-tempered, willful, and morbidly sensitive to criticism or ridicule. His slight lameness was to the end of his life a source of mortification and unhappiness.

Byron was at Trinity College, Cambridge, for two years, and while there brought out his first volume of poems, which met with severe treatment at the hands of the reviewers. Four years later, after months of European travel, he published the

xiv SELECTIONS FOR THE EIGHTH GRADE

first two cantos of "Childe Harold's Pilgrimage," and, as he tells us, woke to find himself famous.

He took his seat in the House of Lords, but soon wearied of politics, and decided to devote himself to literature. His marriage proved to be an unfortunate one, and in 1816 he left England, determined never to return. For eight years he lived abroad, mostly in Italy. In 1824, having had his sympathies deeply stirred by the efforts of the Greeks to free themselves from Turkish rule, he flung himself, heart and soul, into the struggle. He showed great personal bravery, but a sudden illness, due to exposure, brought his short life to an end.

Byron's verse is at its best in his descriptions of natural beauty and grandeur. In its range of expression and in its exquisite phraseology it has rarely been surpassed. Macaulay said of him, "There is not a single note of human anguish of which he is not master;" and yet he never took his work seriously. He despised the very gifts which have made his name famous, and so fell short of what he might have attained. His poetry, like his daily living, had in it a good deal that was flippant and cheap — a sorry contrast to the higher qualities of his nature. Fortunately it is the best literature that lives, and it will be a long time before the glory of Byron's great passages will fade.

Percy Bysshe Shelley was born in Sussex, England, in 1792. His personal inheritance was as fine and sound as Byron's was the reverse, for Shelley was descended from noble families, famous in history and literature. Like Byron, however, he spent his life protesting against the tyranny of social institutions.

As a child he lived in a world of fancy, although he showed remarkable ability in acquiring every kind of knowledge that interested him. He peopled the woods near his home with imaginary dragons and trolls, and hunted for ghosts "through many a listening chamber, cave, and ruin." His first days at school, under a brutal master, roused in him such a fury of revolt against authority that when he entered the preparatory school

INTRODUCTION

of Eton he promptly organized a rebellion against the exactions of the older boys. "Mad Shelley" they called him, but though they tormented the delicate, nervous lad unceasingly, they could not help respecting his pluck and steadfastness.

Unfortunately this harsh and cruel treatment made him so impatient with what he called "the chain of custom" that he came to despise any law which interfered with his personal comfort or pleasure. Before he was able to support himself he took the management of his life into his own hands, and a sad tangle he soon made of it. In spite of his mistakes, however, no one questions the wish to do right or the courage of the young dreamer.

In 1818 Shelley and his wife went to Italy to live. Lord Byron was there at that time, and the two poets saw much of each other. They have sometimes been compared, but neither as men nor as poets were they on the same plane. Notwithstanding his impulsive generosity, Byron was often cynical, careless, and vain; Shelley was an idealist, thirsting after true liberty and beauty. In 1822, while sailing near Leghorn, Shelley was drowned. When his body was washed ashore there was found in his pocket a book written by an English poet whose name has since been often linked with his, and in whose memory one of his greatest poems had been written — John Keats.

Shelley's poetry is full of beautiful images and wonderful melody. Even his passionate protests and sad longings are like strains of fairy music. "To a Skylark," "The West Wind," "Night," and "The Cloud" are the best examples of his lyrical genius.

SELECTED READINGS FOR THE EIGHTH GRADE

THE MAN WITHOUT A COUNTRY

Edward Everett Hale

Note. "This story was written in the summer of 1863, as a contribution however humble, towards the formation of a just and true national sentiment, or sentiment of love to the nation. . . . It is wholly a fiction, 'founded on fact.' The facts on which it is founded are these, — that Aaron Burr sailed down the Mississippi River in 1805, again in 1806, and was tried for treason in 1807. The rest with one exception is all fictitious."

Dr. Hale goes on to explain that when he was collecting material for his story he ran across a reference to a man of the name of Nolan who in the beginning of the last century was killed in Texas. "Finding this mythical character in the mythical legends of a mythical time I took the liberty to give him a cousin, rather more mythical, whose adventures should be upon the seas." Such was the vivid character of the story, however, that for many years its author was frequently obliged to repeat his assertion that it was all pure invention.

The following brief statement, made by Dr. Hale on his eightieth birthday, gives in a few words the lesson he wished to teach. "This was the lesson — that we belong to the State. We cannot help it. We are born into it. . . . My first duty is to the Nation to which I owe my life. . . . This is the reality on which civilized life depends. We bear each other's burdens, and so only we live."

I suppose that very few casual readers of the *New York Herald* of August 13, 1863, observed in an obscure corner, among the "Deaths," the announcement: —

"Nolan. Died, on board U. S. Corvette *Levant*, Lat. 2° 11′ S., Long. 131° W., on the 11th May, Philip Nolan."

I happened to observe it, because I was stranded at the old Mission House in Mackinaw, waiting for a Lake Superior steamer

SELECTIONS FOR THE EIGHTH GRADE

which did not choose to come, and I was devouring to the very stubble all the current literature I could get hold of, even down to the deaths and marriages in the *Herald*. My memory for names and people is good, and the reader will see, as he goes 5 on, that I had reason enough to remember Philip Nolan. There are hundreds of readers who would have paused at that announcement, if the officer of the *Levant* who reported it had chosen to make it thus: "Died, May 11, THE MAN WITHOUT A COUNTRY." For it was as "The Man without a Country" that poor Philip 10 Nolan had generally been known by the officers who had him in charge during some fifty years, as, indeed, by all the men who sailed under them. I dare say that there is many a man who has taken wine with him once a fortnight, in a three years' cruise, who never knew that his name was "Nolan," or whether the 15 poor wretch had any name at all.

There can now be no possible harm in telling this poor creature's story. Reason enough there has been till now, ever since Madison's administration went out in 1817, for very strict secrecy, the secrecy of honor itself, among the gentlemen of the 20 navy who have had Nolan in successive charge. And certainly it speaks well for the *esprit de corps* of the profession, and the personal honor of its members, that to the press this man's story has been wholly unknown — and, I think, to the country at large also. I have some reason to think, from some investigations 25 I made in the Naval Archives when I was attached to the Bureau of Construction, that every official report relating to him was burned when Ross burned the public buildings at Washington. One of the Tuckers, or possibly one of the Watsons, had Nolan in charge at the end of the war; and when, on returning from 30 his cruise, he reported at Washington to one of the Crowninshields — who was in the Navy Department when he came home — he found that the Department ignored the whole business. Whether they really knew nothing about it, or whether it was a "*non mi ricordo*," determined on as a piece of policy, I do not know. But this I do know, that since 1817, and

THE MAN WITHOUT A COUNTRY 3

possibly before, no naval officer has mentioned Nolan in his report of a cruise.

But, as I say, there is no need for secrecy any longer. And now the poor creature is dead, it seems to me worth while to tell a little of his story, by way of showing young Americans of to-day what it is to be A MAN WITHOUT A COUNTRY.

Philip Nolan was as fine a young officer as there was in the "Legion of the West," as the Western division of our army was then called. When Aaron Burr made his first dashing expedition down to New Orleans in 1805, at Fort Massac, or somewhere above on the river, he met, as the Devil would have it, this gay, dashing, bright young fellow; at some dinner party, I think. Burr marked him, talked to him, walked with him, took him a day or two's voyage in his flatboat, and, in short, fascinated him. For the next year barrack life was very tame to poor Nolan. He occasionally availed himself of the permission the great man had given him to write to him. Long, highworded, stilted letters the poor boy wrote and rewrote and copied. But never a line did he have in reply from the gay deceiver. The other boys in the garrison sneered at him, because he lost the fun which they found in shooting or rowing while he was working away on these grand letters to his grand friend. They could not understand why Nolan kept by himself while they were playing high-low jack. Poker was not yet invented. But before long the young fellow had his revenge. For this time his Excellency, the Honorable Aaron Burr, appeared again under a very different aspect. There were rumors that he had an army behind him, and everybody supposed that he had an empire before him. At that time the youngsters all envied him. Burr had not been talking twenty minutes with the commander before he asked him to send for Lieutenant Nolan. Then, after a little talk, he asked Nolan if he could show him something of the great river and the plans for the new post. He asked Nolan to take him out in his skiff, to show him a canebrake or a cottonwood tree, as he said — really

4 SELECTIONS FOR THE EIGHTH GRADE

to seduce him; and by the time the sail was over Nolan was enlisted, body and soul. From that time, although he did not yet know it, he lived as A MAN WITHOUT A COUNTRY.

What Burr meant to do I know no more than you, dear
5 reader. It is none of our business just now. Only, when the grand catastrophe came, and Jefferson and the House of Virginia of that day undertook to break on the wheel all the possible Clarences of the then House of York, by the great treason trial at Richmond, some of the lesser fry in that distant Mississippi
10 Valley, which was farther from us than Puget's Sound is to-day, introduced the like novelty on their provincial stage; and, to while away the monotony of the summer at Fort Adams, got up, for *spectacles*, a string of courts-martial on the officers there. One and another of the colonels and majors were tried, and, to
15 fill out the list, little Nolan, against whom, Heaven knows, there was evidence enough — that he was sick of the service, had been willing to be false to it, and would have obeyed any order to march any-whither with any one who would follow him had the order been signed, "By command of his Exc. A.
20 Burr." The courts dragged on. The big flies escaped — rightfully for all I know. Nolan was proved guilty enough, as I say; yet you and I would never have heard of him, reader, but that, when the president of the court asked him at the close whether he wished to say anything to show that he had
25 always been faithful to the United States, he cried out, in a fit of frenzy: —

"Damn the United States! I wish I may never hear of the United States again!"

I suppose he did not know how the words shocked old Colonel
30 Morgan, who was holding the court. Half the officers who sat in it had served through the Revolution, and their lives, not to say their necks, had been risked for the very idea which he so cavalierly cursed in his madness. He, on his part, had grown up in the West of those days, in the midst of "Spanish plot," "Orleans plot," and all the rest. He had been educated on a

THE MAN WITHOUT A COUNTRY

plantation where the finest company was a Spanish officer or a French merchant from Orleans. His education, such as it was, had been perfected in commercial expeditions to Vera Cruz, and I think he told me his father once hired an Englishman to be a private tutor for a winter on the plantation. He had spent 5 half his youth with an older brother, hunting horses in Texas; and, in a word, to him "United States" was scarcely a reality. Yet he had been fed by "United States" for all the years since he had been in the army. He had sworn on his faith as a Christian to be true to "United States." It was "United 10 States" which gave him the uniform he wore, and the sword by his side. Nay, my poor Nolan, it was only because "United States" had picked you out first as one of her own confidential men of honor that "A. Burr" cared for you a straw more than for the flatboat men who sailed his ark for him. I do not ex-15 cuse Nolan; I only explain to the reader why he damned his country, and wished he might never hear her name again.

He never did hear her name but once again. From that moment, September 23, 1807, till the day he died, May 11, 1863, he never heard her name again. For that half century 20 and more he was a man without a country.

Old Morgan, as I said, was terribly shocked. If Nolan had compared George Washington to Benedict Arnold, or had cried, "God save King George," Morgan would not have felt worse. He called the Court into his private room, and returned in 25 fifteen minutes, with a face like a sheet, to say: —

"Prisoner, hear the sentence of the Court! The Court decides, subject to the approval of the President, that you never hear the name of the United States again."

Nolan laughed. But nobody else laughed. Old Morgan was 30 too solemn, and the whole room was hushed dead as night for a minute. Even Nolan lost his swagger in a moment. Then Morgan added: —

"Mr. Marshal, take the prisoner to Orleans in an armed boat, and deliver him to the naval commander there."

6   SELECTIONS FOR THE EIGHTH GRADE

The marshal gave his orders and the prisoner was taken out of court.

"Mr. Marshal," continued old Morgan, "see that no one mentions the United States to the prisoner. Mr. Marshal, 5 make my respects to Lieutenant Mitchell at Orleans, and request him to order that no one shall mention the United States to the prisoner while he is on board ship. You will receive your written orders from the officer on duty here this evening. The court is adjourned without day."

10 I have always supposed that Colonel Morgan himself took the proceedings of the court to Washington city, and explained them to Mr. Jefferson. Certain it is that the President approved them — certain, that is, if I may believe the men who say they have seen his signature. Before the *Nautilus* got 15 round from New Orleans to the Northern Atlantic coast with the prisoner on board, the sentence had been approved, and he was a man without a country.

The plan then adopted was substantially the same which was necessarily followed ever after. Perhaps it was suggested 20 by the necessity of sending him by water from Fort Adams and Orleans. The Secretary of the Navy — it must have been the first Crowninshield, though he is a man I do not remember — was requested to put Nolan on board a Government vessel bound on a long cruise, and to direct that he should be only so 25 far confined there as to make it certain that he never saw or heard of the country. We had few long cruises then, and the navy was very much out of favor; and, as almost all of this story is traditional, as I have explained, I do not know certainly what his first cruise was. But the commander to whom he was 30 intrusted — perhaps it was Tingey or Shaw, though I think it was one of the younger men — we are all old enough now — regulated the etiquette and the precautions of the affair, and according to his scheme they were carried out, I suppose, till Nolan died.

When I was second officer of the *Intrepid*, some thirty years

THE MAN WITHOUT A COUNTRY

after, I saw the original paper of instructions. I have been sorry ever since that I did not copy the whole of it. It ran, however, much in this way: —

> "Washington (with a date, which must have been late in 1807)

"SIR: — You will receive from Lieutenant Neale the person of Philip Nolan, late a lieutenant in the United States army.

"This person on his trial by court-martial expressed, with an oath, the wish that he might 'never hear of the United States again.'

"The Court sentenced him to have his wish fulfilled.

"For the present, the execution of the order is intrusted by the President to this Department.

"You will take the prisoner on board your ship and keep him there with such precautions as shall prevent his escape.

"You will provide him with such quarters, rations, and clothing as would be proper for an officer of his late rank, if he were a passenger on your vessel on the business of his Government.

"The gentlemen on board will make any arrangements agreeable to themselves regarding his society. He is to be exposed to no indignity of any kind, nor is he ever unnecessarily to be reminded that he is a prisoner.

"But under no circumstances is he ever to hear of his country or to see any information regarding it; and you will especially caution all the officers under your command to take care that, in the various indulgences which may be granted, this rule, in which his punishment is involved, shall not be broken.

"It is the intention of the Government that he shall never again see the country which he has disowned. Before the end of your cruise you will receive orders which will give effect to this intention.

> "Respectfully yours,
> W. SOUTHARD, for the
> Secretary of the Navy"

8 SELECTIONS FOR THE EIGHTH GRADE

If I had only preserved the whole of this paper, there would be no break in the beginning of my sketch of this story. For Captain Shaw, if it were he, handed it to his successor in the charge, and he to his, and I suppose the commander of the 5 *Levant* has it to-day as his authority for keeping this man in this mild custody.

The rule adopted on board the ships on which I have met "the man without a country" was, I think, transmitted from the beginning. No mess liked to have him permanently, be-10 cause his presence cut off all talk of home or of the prospect of return, of politics or letters, of peace or of war — cut off more than half the talk men like to have at sea. But it was always thought too hard that he should never meet the rest of us, except to touch hats, and we finally sank into one system. He 15 was not permitted to talk with the men, unless an officer was by. With officers he had unrestrained intercourse, as far as they and he chose. But he grew shy, though he had favorites: I was one. Then the captain always asked him to dinner on Monday. Every mess in succession took up the invitation in 20 its turn. According to the size of the ship, you had him at your mess more or less often at dinner. His breakfast he ate in his own stateroom — he always had a stateroom — which was where a sentinel or somebody on the watch could see the door. And whatever else he ate or drank, he ate or drank 25 alone. Sometimes, when the marines or sailors had any special jollification, they were permitted to invite "Plain-Buttons," as they called him. Then Nolan was sent with some officer, and the men were forbidden to speak of home while he was there. I believe the theory was that the sight of his punishment did 30 them good. They called him "Plain-Buttons" because, while he always chose to wear a regulation army uniform, he was not permitted to wear the army button, for the reason that it bore either the initials or the insignia of the country he had disowned.

I remember, soon after I joined the navy, I was on shore with some of the older officers from our ship and from the

THE MAN WITHOUT A COUNTRY

Brandywine, which we had met at Alexandria. We had leave to make a party and go up to Cairo and the Pyramids. As we jogged along (you went on donkeys then), some of the gentlemen (we boys called them "Dons," but the phrase was long since changed) fell to talking about Nolan, and some one told 5 the system which was adopted from the first about his books and other reading. As he was almost never permitted to go on shore, even though the vessel lay in port for months, his time at the best hung heavy; and everybody was permitted to lend him books, if they were not published in America and 10 made no allusion to it. These were common enough in the old days, when people in the other hemisphere talked of the United States as little as we do of Paraguay. He had almost all the foreign papers that came into the ship, sooner or later; only somebody must go over them first, and cut out any advertise- 15 ment or stray paragraph that alluded to America. This was a little cruel sometimes, when the back of what was cut out might be as innocent as Hesiod. Right in the midst of one of Napoleon's battles, or one of Canning's speeches, poor Nolan would find a great hole, because on the back of the page of that 20 paper there had been an advertisement of a packet for New York, or a scrap from the President's Message. I say this was the first time I ever heard of this plan, which afterwards I had enough and more than enough to do with. I remember it, because poor Phillips, who was of the party, as soon as the 25 allusion to reading was made, told a story of something which happened at the Cape of Good Hope on Nolan's first voyage; and it is the only thing I ever knew of that voyage. They had touched at the Cape, and had done the civil thing with the English Admiral and the fleet, and then, leaving for a long cruise 30 up the Indian Ocean, Phillips had borrowed a lot of English books from an officer, which, in those days, as indeed in these, was quite a windfall. Among them, as the Devil would order, was "The Lay of the Last Minstrel," which they had all of them heard of, but which most of them had never seen. I

SELECTIONS FOR THE EIGHTH GRADE

think it could not have been published long. Well, nobody thought there could be any risk of anything national in that, though Phillips swore old Shaw had cut out "The Tempest" from Shakespeare before he let Nolan have it, because he said "the Bermudas ought to be ours, and, by Jove, should be, one day." So Nolan was permitted to join the circle one afternoon when a lot of them sat on deck smoking and reading aloud. People do not do such things so often now; but when I was young we got rid of a great deal of time so. Well, so it happened that in his turn Nolan took the book and read to the others; and he read very well, as I know. Nobody in the circle knew a line of the poem, only it was all magic and Border chivalry, and was ten thousand years ago. Poor Nolan read steadily through the fifth canto, stopped a minute and drank something, and then began, without a thought of what was coming : —

> "Breathes there the man, with soul so dead,
> Who never to himself hath said" —

It seems impossible to us that anybody ever heard this for the first time; but all these fellows did then, and poor Nolan himself went on, still unconsciously or mechanically —

> "This is my own, my native land!"

Then they all saw that something was to pay; but he expected to get through, I suppose, turned a little pale, but plunged on —

> "Whose heart hath ne'er within him burned,
> As home his footsteps he hath turned
> From wandering on a foreign strand?
> If such there breathe, go, mark him well" —

By this time the men were all beside themselves, wishing there was any way to make him turn over two pages; but he had not quite presence of mind for that; he gagged a little, colored crimson, and staggered on —

THE MAN WITHOUT A COUNTRY

"For him no minstrel raptures swell;
High though his titles, proud his name,
Boundless his wealth as wish can claim,
Despite these titles, power, and pelf,
The wretch, concentered all in self" —

and here the poor fellow choked, could not go on, but started up, swung the book into the sea, vanished into his stateroom, "And, by Jove," said Phillips, "we did not see him for two months again. And I had to make up some beggarly story to that English surgeon why I did not return his Walter Scott to him."

That story shows about the time when Nolan's braggadocio must have broken down. At first, they said, he took a very high tone, considered his imprisonment a mere farce, affected to enjoy the voyage, and all that; but Phillips said that after he came out of his stateroom he never was the same man again. He never read aloud again, unless it was the Bible or Shakespeare, or something else he was sure of. But it was not that merely. He never entered in with the other young men exactly as a companion again. He was always shy afterwards, when I knew him — very seldom spoke, unless he was spoken to, except to a very few friends. He lighted up occasionally — I remember late in his life hearing him fairly eloquent on something which had been suggested to him by one of Fléchier's sermons — but generally he had the nervous, tired look of a heart-wounded man.

When Captain Shaw was coming home — if, as I say, it was Shaw — rather to the surprise of everybody they made one of the Windward Islands, and lay off and on for nearly a week. The boys said the officers were sick of salt junk, and meant to have turtle soup before they came home. But after several days the *Warren* came to the same rendezvous; they exchanged signals; she sent to Phillips and these homeward-bound men letters and papers, and told them she was outward-bound, perhaps to the Mediterranean, and took poor Nolan and his traps

12 SELECTIONS FOR THE EIGHTH GRADE

on the boat back to try his second cruise. He looked very blank when he was told to get ready to join her. He had known enough of the signs of the sky to know that till that moment he was going "home." But this was a distinct evidence of
5 something he had not thought of, perhaps — that there was no going home for him, even to a prison. And this was the first of some twenty such transfers, which brought him sooner or later into half our best vessels, but which kept him all his life at least some hundred miles from the country he had hoped
10 he might never hear of again.

It may have been on that second cruise — it was once when he was up the Mediterranean — that Mrs. Graff, the celebrated Southern beauty of those days, danced with him. They had been lying a long time in the Bay of Naples, and the officers
15 were very intimate in the English fleet, and there had been great festivities, and our men thought they must give a great ball on board the ship. How they ever did it on board the *Warren* I am sure I do not know. Perhaps it was not the *Warren*, or perhaps ladies did not take up so much room as they do now.
20 They wanted to use Nolan's stateroom for something, and they hated to do it without asking him to the ball; so the captain said they might ask him, if they would be responsible that he did not talk with the wrong people, "who would give him intelligence." So the dance went on, the finest party that had
25 ever been known, I dare say; for I never heard of a man-of-war ball that was not. For ladies they had the family of the ` American consul, one or two travelers who had adventured so far, and a nice bevy of English girls and matrons, perhaps Lady Hamilton herself.

30 Well, different officers relieved each other in standing and talking with Nolan in a friendly way, so as to be sure that nobody else spoke to him. The dancing went on with spirit, and after a while even the fellows who took this honorary guard of Nolan ceased to fear any *contretemps*. Only when some English lady — Lady Hamilton, as I said, perhaps — called for a

THE MAN WITHOUT A COUNTRY 13

set of "American dances," an odd thing happened. Everybody then danced contra-dances. The black band, nothing loth, conferred as to what "American dances" were, and started off with "Virginia Reel," which they followed with "Money-Musk," which, in its turn in those days, should have been followed by "The Old Thirteen." But just as Dick, the leader, tapped for his fiddles to begin, and bent forward, about to say in true negro state, "'The Old Thirteen,' gentlemen and ladies!" as he had said "'Virginny Reel,' if you please!" and "'Money-Musk,' if you please!" the captain's boy tapped him on the shoulder, whispered to him, and he did not announce the name of the dance; he merely bowed, began on the air, and they all fell to — the officers teaching the English girls the figure, but not telling them why it had no name.

But that is not the story I started to tell. As the dancing went on, Nolan and our fellows all got at ease, as I said — so much so that it seemed quite natural for him to bow to that splendid Mrs. Graff and say: —

"I hope you have not forgotten me, Miss Rutledge. Shall I have the honor of dancing?"

He did it so quickly that Fellows, who was with him, could not hinder him. She laughed and said: —

"I am not Miss Rutledge any longer, Mr. Nolan; but I will dance all the same," just nodded to Fellows, as if to say he must leave Mr. Nolan to her, and led him off to the place where the dance was forming.

Nolan thought he had got his chance. He had known her at Philadelphia, and at other places had met her, and this was a godsend. You could not talk in contra-dances, as you do in cotillions, or even in the pauses of waltzing; but there were chances for tongues and sounds, as well as for eyes and blushes. He began with her travels, and Europe, and Vesuvius, and the French; and then, when they had worked down, and had that long talking time at the bottom of the set, he said boldly — a little pale, she said, as she told me the story years after: —

SELECTIONS FOR THE EIGHTH GRADE

"And what do you hear from home, Mrs. Graff?"

And that splendid creature looked through him. Jove! how she must have looked through him!

"Home!! Mr. Nolan!!! I thought you were the man
5 who never wanted to hear of home again!" — and she walked directly up the deck to her husband, and left poor Nolan alone, as he always was. He did not dance again. I cannot give any history of him in order; nobody can now; and, indeed, I am not trying to.

10 These are the traditions, which I sort out, as I believe them, from the myths which have been told about this man for forty years. The lies that have been told about him are legion. The fellows used to say he was the "Iron Mask"; and poor George Pons went to his grave in the belief that this was the
15 author of "Junius," who was being punished for his celebrated libel on Thomas Jefferson. Pons was not very strong in the historical line.

A happier story than either of these I have told is of the war. That came along soon after. I have heard this affair
20 told in three or four ways — and, indeed, it may have happened more than once. But which ship it was on I cannot tell. However, in one, at least, of the great frigate duels with the English, in which the navy was really baptized, it happened that a round-shot from the enemy entered one of our ports square,
25 and took right down the officer of the gun himself, and almost every man of the gun crew. Now you may say what you choose about courage, but that is not a nice thing to see. But, as the men who were not killed picked themselves up, and as they and the surgeon's people were carrying off the bodies, there
30 appeared Nolan, in his shirt-sleeves, with the rammer in his hand, and, just as if he had been the officer, told them off with authority — who should go to the cockpit with the wounded men, who should stay with him — perfectly cheery, and with that way which makes men feel sure all is right and is going to be right. And he finished loading the gun with his own

THE MAN WITHOUT A COUNTRY 15

hands, aimed it, and bade the men fire. And there he stayed, captain of that gun, keeping those fellows in spirits, till the enemy struck — sitting on the carriage while the gun was cooling, though he was exposed all the time — showing them easier ways to handle heavy shot — making the raw hands laugh at their own blunders — and when the gun cooled again, getting it loaded and fired twice as often as any other gun on the ship. The captain walked forward by way of encouraging the men, and Nolan touched his hat and said: —

"I am showing them how we do this in the artillery, sir."

And this is the part of the story where all the legends agree; the commodore said: —

"I see you do, and I thank you, sir; and I shall never forget this day, sir, and you never shall, sir."

And after the whole thing was over, and he had the Englishman's sword, in the midst of the state and ceremony of the quarter-deck, he said: —

"Where is Mr. Nolan? Ask Mr. Nolan to come here."

And when Nolan came, he said: —

"Mr. Nolan, we are all very grateful to you to-day; you are one of us to-day; you will be named in the dispatches."

And then the old man took off his own sword of ceremony and gave it to Nolan, and made him put it on. The man told me this who saw it. Nolan cried like a baby, and well he might. He had not worn a sword since that infernal day at Fort Adams. But always afterwards on occasions of ceremony he wore that quaint old French sword of the commodore's.

The captain did mention him in the dispatches. It was always said he asked that he might be pardoned. He wrote a special letter to the Secretary of War. But nothing ever came of it. As I said, that was about the time when they began to ignore the whole transaction at Washington, and when Nolan's imprisonment began to carry itself on because there was nobody to stop it without any new orders from home.

I have heard it said that he was with Porter when he took

16 SELECTIONS FOR THE EIGHTH GRADE

possession of the Nukahiwa Islands. Not this Porter, you know, but old Porter, his father, Essex Porter — that is, the old Essex Porter, not this Essex. As an artillery officer, who had seen service in the West, Nolan knew more about fortifications,
5 embrasures, ravelins, stockades, and all that, than any of them did; and he worked with a right good will in fixing that battery all right. I have always thought it was a pity Porter did not leave him in command there with Gamble. That would have settled all the question about his punishment. We should have
10 kept the islands, and at this moment we should have one station in the Pacific Ocean. Our French friends, too, when they wanted this little watering place, would have found it was preoccupied. But Madison and the Virginians, of course, flung all that away.
15 All that was near fifty years ago. If Nolan was thirty then, he must have been near eighty when he died. He looked sixty when he was forty. But he never seemed to me to change a hair afterwards. As I imagine his life, from what I have seen and heard of it, he must have been in every sea, and yet almost
20 never on land. He must have known, in a formal way, more officers in our service than any man living knows. He told me once, with a grave smile, that no man in the world lived so methodical a life as he. "You know the boys say I am the Iron Mask, and you know how busy he was." He said it did not do
25 for any one to try to read all the time, more than to do anything else all the time; and that he used to read just five hours a day. "Then," he said, "I keep up my notebooks, writing in them at such and such hours from what I have been reading; and I include in these my scrapbooks." These were very curi-
30 ous indeed. He had six or eight, of different subjects. There was one of History, one of Natural Science, one which he called "Odds and Ends." But they were not merely books of extracts from newspapers. They had bits of plants and ribbons, shells tied on, and carved scraps of bone and wood, which he had taught the men to cut for him, and they were beautifully

THE MAN WITHOUT A COUNTRY 17

illustrated. He drew admirably. He had some of the funniest drawings there, and some of the most pathetic, that I have ever seen in my life. I wonder who will have Nolan's scrap books.

Well, he said his reading and his notes were his profession, and that they took five hours and two hours respectively of each day. "Then," said he, "every man should have a diversion as well as a profession. My Natural History is my diversion." That took two hours a day more. The men used to bring him birds and fish, but on a long cruise he had to satisfy himself with centipedes and cockroaches and such small game. He was the only naturalist I ever met who knew anything about the habits of the house fly and the mosquito. All those people can tell you whether they are *Lepidoptera* or *Steptopotera;* but as for telling how you can get rid of them, or how they can get away from you when you strike them — why, Linnæus knew as little of that as John Foy the idiot did. These nine hours made Nolan's regular daily "occupation." The rest of the time he talked or walked. Till he grew very old, he went aloft a great deal. He always kept up his exercise; and I never heard that he was ill. If any other man was ill, he was the kindest nurse in the world; and he knew more than half the surgeons do. Then if anybody was sick or died, or if the captain wanted him to, on any other occasion, he was always ready to read prayers. I have said that he read beautifully.

My own acquaintance with Philip Nolan began six or eight years after the English war, on my first voyage after I was appointed a midshipman. It was in the first days after our Slave Trade treaty, while the Reigning House, which was still the House of Virginia, had still a sort of sentimentalism about the suppression of the horrors of the Middle Passage, and something was sometimes done that way. We were in the South Atlantic on that business. From the time I joined, I believe I thought Nolan was a sort of lay chaplain — a chaplain with a blue coat. I never asked about him. Everything in the ship was strange to me. I knew it was green to ask

18   SELECTIONS FOR THE EIGHTH GRADE

questions, and I suppose I thought there was a "Plain-Buttons" on every ship. We had him to dine in our mess once a week, and the caution was given that on that day nothing was to be said about home. But if they had told us not to say anything 5 about the planet Mars or the Book of Deuteronomy, I should not have asked why; there were a great many things which seemed to me to have as little reason. I first came to understand anything about the "man without a country" one day when we overhauled a dirty little schooner which had slaves 10 on board. An officer was sent to take charge of her, and, after a few minutes, he sent back his boat to ask that some one might be sent him who could speak Portuguese. We were all looking over the rail when the message came, and we all wished we could interpret, when the captain asked who spoke Portu- 15 guese. But none of the officers did; and just as the captain was sending forward to ask if any of the people could, Nolan stepped out and said he should be glad to interpret, if the captain wished, as he understood the language. The captain thanked him, fitted out another boat with him, and in this 20 boat it was my luck to go.

When we got there, it was such a scene as you seldom see, and never want to. Nastiness beyond account, and chaos run loose in the midst of the nastiness. There were not a great many of the negroes; but by way of making what there were 25 understand that they were free, Vaughan had had their handcuffs and ankle cuffs knocked off, and, for convenience' sake, was putting them upon the rascals of the schooner's crew. The negroes were, most of them, out of the hold, and swarming all around the dirty deck, with a central throng surround- 30 ing Vaughan and addressing him in every dialect, and *patois* of a dialect, from the Zulu click up to the Parisian of Beledeljereed.

As we came on deck, Vaughan looked down from a hogshead, on which he had mounted in desperation, and said: —

"For God's love, is there anybody who can make these wretches understand something? The men gave them rum,

THE MAN WITHOUT A COUNTRY 19

and that did not quiet them. I knocked that big fellow down twice, and that did not soothe him. And then I talked Choctaw to all of them together; and I'll be hanged if they understood that as well as they understood the English."

Nolan said he could speak Portuguese, and one or two fine-looking Kroomen were dragged out, who, as it had been found already, had worked for the Portuguese on the coast at Fernando Po.

"Tell them they are free," said Vaughan; "and tell them that these rascals are to be hanged as soon as we can get rope enough."

Nolan "put that into Spanish" — that is, he explained it in such Portuguese as the Kroomen could understand, and they in turn to such of the negroes as could understand them. Then there was such a yell of delight, clinching of the fists, leaping and dancing, kissing of Nolan's feet, and a general rush made to the hogshead by way of spontaneous worship of Vaughan, as the *deus ex machina* of the occasion.

"Tell them," said Vaughan, well pleased, "that I will take them all to Cape Palmas."

This did not answer so well. Cape Palmas was practically as far from the homes of most of them as New Orleans or Rio Janeiro was; that is, they would be eternally separated from home there. And their interpreters, as we could understand, instantly said, "*Ah, non Palmas*," and began to propose infinite other expedients in most voluble language. Vaughan was rather disappointed at this result of his liberality, and asked Nolan eagerly what they said. The drops stood on poor Nolan's white forehead, as he hushed the men down, and said:

"He says, 'Not Palmas.' He says, 'Take us home, take us to our own country, take us to our own house, take us to our own pickaninnies and our own women.' He says he has an old father and mother who will die if they do not see him. And this one says he left his people all sick, and paddled down to Fernando to beg the white doctor to come and help them, and

20 SELECTIONS FOR THE EIGHTH GRADE

that these devils caught him in the bay just in sight of home, and that he has never seen anybody from home since then. And this one says," choked out Nolan, "that he has not heard a word from his home in six months, while he has been locked
5 up in an infernal barracoon."

Vaughan always said he grew gray himself while Nolan struggled through this interpretation. I, who did not understand anything of the passion involved in it, saw that the very elements were melting with fervent heat, and that some-
10 thing was to pay somewhere. Even the negroes themselves stopped howling, as they saw Nolan's agony and Vaughan's almost equal agony of sympathy. As quick as he could get words, he said: —

"Tell them yes, yes, yes; tell them they shall go to the
15 Mountains of the Moon, if they will. If I sail the schooner through the Great White Desert, they shall go home!"

And after some fashion Nolan said so. And then they all fell to kissing him again, and wanted to rub his nose with theirs.
20 But he could not stand it long; and, getting Vaughan to say he might go back, he beckoned me down into our boat. As we lay back in the stern sheets and the men gave way, he said to me: "Youngster, let that show you what it is to be without a family, without a home, and without a country. And if you
25 are ever tempted to say a word or to do a thing that shall put a bar between you and your family, your home, and your country, pray God in his mercy to take you that instant home to his own heaven. Stick by your family, boy; forget you have a self, while you do everything for them. Think of your home, boy;
30 write and send and talk about it. Let it be nearer and nearer to your thought the farther you have to travel from it; and rush back to it when you are free, as that poor black slave is doing now. And for your country, boy," and the words rattled in his throat, "and for that flag," and he pointed to the ship, "never dream a dream but of serving her as she bids you, though

THE MAN WITHOUT A COUNTRY

the service carry you through a thousand hells. No matter what happens to you, no matter who flatters you or who abuses you, never look at another flag, never let a night pass but you pray God to bless that flag. Remember, boy, that behind all these men you have to do with, behind officers, and Government, and people even, there is the Country Herself, your Country, and that you belong to Her as you belong to your own mother. Stand by Her, boy, as you would stand by your mother, if those devils there had got hold of her to-day!"

I was frightened to death by his calm, hard passion; but I blundered out that I would, by all that was holy, and that I had never thought of doing anything else. He hardly seemed to hear me; but he did, almost in a whisper, say, "Oh, if anybody had said so to me when I was of your age!"

I think it was this half confidence of his, which I never abused, for I never told this story till now, which afterward made us great friends. He was very kind to me. Often he sat up, or even got up, at night to walk the deck with me when it was my watch. He explained to me a great deal of my mathematics, and I owe to him my taste for mathematics. He lent me books, and helped me about my reading. He never alluded so directly to his story again; but from one and another officer I have learned, in thirty years, what I am telling. When we parted from him in St. Thomas harbor, at the end of our cruise, I was more sorry than I can tell. I was very glad to meet him again in 1830; and later in life, when I thought I had some influence in Washington, I moved heaven and earth to have him discharged. But it was like getting a ghost out of prison. They pretended there was no such man, and never was such a man. They will say so at the Department now! Perhaps they do not know. It will not be the first thing in the service of which the Department appears to know nothing!

There is a story that Nolan met Burr once on one of our vessels, when a party of Americans came on board in the Mediterranean. But this I believe to be a lie; or, rather, it is a myth,

22 SELECTIONS FOR THE EIGHTH GRADE

ben trovato, involving a tremendous blowing-up with which he sunk Burr — asking him how he liked to be "without a country." But it is clear from Burr's life that nothing of the sort could have happened; and I mention this only as an illustration of the sto-
5 ries which get a-going where there is the least mystery at bottom.

So poor Philip Nolan had his wish fulfilled. I know but one fate more dreadful; it is the fate reserved for those men who shall have one day to exile themselves from their country because they have attempted her ruin, and shall have at the same time
10 to see the prosperity and honor to which she rises when she has rid herself of them and their iniquities. The wish of poor Nolan, as we all learned to call him, not because his punishment was too great, but because his repentance was so clear, was precisely the wish of every Bragg and Beauregard who broke a
15 soldier's oath two years ago, and of every Maury and Barron who broke a sailor's. I do not know how often they have repented. I do know that they have done all that in them lay that they might have no country — that all the honors, associations, memories, and hopes which belong to "coun-
20 try" might be broken up into little shreds and distributed to the winds. I know, too, that their punishment, as they vegetate through what is left of life to them in wretched Boulognes and Leicester Squares, where they are destined to upbraid each other till they die, will have all the agony of Nolan's,
25 with the added pang that every one who sees them will see them to despise and to execrate them. They will have their wish, like him.

For him, poor fellow, he repented of his folly, and then, like a man, submitted to the fate he had asked for. He never inten-
30 tionally added to the difficulty or delicacy of the charge of those who had him in hold. Accidents would happen; but they never happened from his fault. Lieutenant Truxton told me that, when Texas was annexed, there was a careful discussion among the officers whether they should get hold of Nolan's handsome set of maps and cut Texas out of it — from the map of the world

THE MAN WITHOUT A COUNTRY 23

and the map of Mexico. The United States had been cut out when the atlas was bought for him. But it was voted, rightly enough, that to do this would be virtually to reveal to him what had happened, or, as Harry Cole said, to make him think Old Burr had succeeded. So it was from no fault of Nolan's that a great botch happened at my own table, when, for a short time, I was in command of the George Washington corvette, on the South American station. We were lying in the La Plata, and some of the officers, who had been on shore and had just joined again, were entertaining us with an account of their misadventures in riding the half-wild horses of Buenos Aires. Nolan was at table, and was in an unusually bright and talkative mood. Some story of a tumble reminded him of an adventure of his own when he was catching wild horses in Texas with his adventurous cousin, at a time when he must have been quite a boy. He told the story with a good deal of spirit — so much so that the silence which often follows a good story hung over the table for an instant, to be broken by Nolan himself. For he asked, perfectly unconsciously:

"Pray, what has become of Texas? After the Mexicans got their independence, I thought that province of Texas would come forward very fast. It is really one of the finest regions on earth; it is the Italy of this continent. But I have not seen or heard a word of Texas for near twenty years."

There were two Texan officers at the table. The reason he had never heard of Texas was that Texas and her affairs had been painfully cut out of his newspapers since Austin began his settlements; so that, while he read of Honduras and Tamaulipas, and, till quite lately, of California —·this virgin province, in which his brother had traveled so far, and, I believe, had died, had ceased to be to him. Waters and Williams, the two Texas men, looked grimly at each other and tried not to laugh. Edward Morris had his attention attracted by the third link in the chain of the captain's chandelier. Watrous was seized with a fit of sneezing. Nolan himself saw that something was to pay,

24   SELECTIONS FOR THE EIGHTH GRADE

he did not know what. And I, as master of the feast, had to say : —

"Texas is out of the map, Mr. Nolan. Have you seen Captain Back's curious account of Sir Thomas Roe's Welcome?"

After that cruise I never saw Nolan again. I wrote to him at least twice a year, for in that voyage we became even confidentially intimate; but he never wrote to me. The other men tell me that in those fifteen years he *aged* very fast, as well he might indeed, but that he was still the same gentle, uncomplaining, silent sufferer that he ever was, bearing as best he could his self-appointed punishment — rather less social, perhaps, with new men whom he did not know, but more anxious, apparently, than ever to serve and befriend and teach the boys, some of whom fairly seemed to worship him. And now it seems the dear old fellow is dead. He has found a home at last, and a country.

Since writing this, and while considering whether or no I would print it, as a warning to the young Nolans and Vallandighams and Tatnalls of to-day of what it is to throw away a country, I have received from Danforth, who is on board the *Levant*, a letter which gives an account of Nolan's last hours. It removes all my doubts about telling this story.

The reader will understand Danforth's letter, or the beginning of it, if he will remember that after ten years of Nolan's exile every one who had him in charge was in a very delicate position. The Government had failed to renew the order of 1807 regarding him. What was a man to do? Should he let him go? What, then, if he were called to account by the Department for violating the order of 1807? Should he keep him? What, then, if Nolan should be liberated some day, and should bring an action for false imprisonment or kidnaping against every man who had had him in charge? I urged and pressed this upon Southard, and I have reason to think that other officers did the same thing. But the Secretary always said, as they so often do at Washington, that there were no special orders to give, and that we must act on our own judgment. That means, "If you succeed, you

THE MAN WITHOUT A COUNTRY · 25

will be sustained; if you fail, you will be disavowed." Well, as Danforth says, all that is over now, though I do not know but I expose myself to a criminal prosecution on the evidence of the very revelation I am making.

Here is the letter: —

"Levant, 2° 2' S. @ 131° W.

"DEAR FRED: — I try to find heart and life to tell you that it is all over with dear old Nolan. I have been with him on this voyage more than I ever was, and I can understand wholly now the way in which you used to speak of the dear old fellow. I could see that he was not strong, but I had no idea the end was so near. The doctor has been watching him very carefully, and yesterday morning came to me and told me that Nolan was not so well, and had not left his stateroom — a thing I never remember before. He had let the doctor come and see him as he lay there — the first time the doctor had been in the stateroom — and he said he should like to see me. Oh, dear! do you remember the mysteries we boys used to invent about his room in the old *Intrepid* days? Well, I went in, and there, to be sure, the poor fellow lay in his berth, smiling pleasantly as he gave me his hand, but looking very frail. I could not help a glance round, which showed me what a little shrine he had made of the box he was lying in. The Stars and Stripes were triced up above and around a picture of Washington, and he had painted a majestic eagle, with lightnings blazing from his beak and his foot just clasping the whole globe, which his wings overshadowed. The dear old boy saw my glance, and said, with a sad smile, 'Here, you see, I have a country!' And then he pointed to the foot of his bed, where I had not seen before a great map of the United States, as he had drawn it from memory, and which he had there to look upon as he lay. Quaint, queer old names were on it, in large letters: 'Indiana Territory,' 'Mississippi Territory,' and 'Louisiana Territory,' as I suppose our fathers learned such things: but the old fellow had patched in Texas, too; he

26 SELECTIONS FOR THE EIGHTH GRADE

had carried his western boundary all the way to the Pacific, but on that shore he had defined nothing.

"'O Danforth!' he said, 'I know I am dying. I cannot get home. Surely you will tell me something now? — Stop! stop! do not speak till I say what I am sure you know, that there is not in this ship, that there is not in America — God bless her! — a more loyal man than I. There cannot be a man who loves the old flag as I do, or prays for it as I do, or hopes for it as I do. There are thirty-four stars in it now, Danforth. I thank God for that, though I do not know what their names are. There has never been one taken away: I thank God for that. I know by that that there has never been any successful Burr. O Danforth, Danforth,' he sighed out, 'how like a wretched night's dream a boy's idea of personal fame or of separate sovereignty seems, when one looks back on it after such a life as mine! But tell me — tell me something — tell me everything, Danforth, before I die!'

"Ingham, I swear to you that I felt like a monster that I had not told him everything before. Danger or no danger, delicacy or no delicacy, who was I, that I should have been acting the tyrant all this time over this dear, sainted old man, who had years ago expiated, in his whole manhood's life, the madness of a boy's treason? 'Mr. Nolan,' said I, 'I will tell you everything you ask about. Only, where shall I begin?'

"Oh, the blessed smile that crept over his white face! and he pressed my hand and said, 'God bless you! Tell me their names,' he said, and he pointed to the stars on the flag. 'The last I know is Ohio. My father lived in Kentucky. But I have guessed Michigan and Indiana and Mississippi — that was where Fort Adams is — they make twenty. But where are your other fourteen? You have not cut up any of the old ones, I hope?'

"Well, that was not a bad text, and I told him the names in as good order as I could, and he bade me take down his beautiful map and draw them in as I best could with my pencil. He was wild with delight about Texas, told me how his cousin died there;

THE MAN WITHOUT A COUNTRY 27

he had marked a gold cross near where he supposed his grave was; and he had guessed at Texas. Then he was delighted as he saw California and Oregon; that, he said, he had suspected partly, because he had never been permitted to land on that shore, though the ships were there so much. 'And the men,' said he, 5 laughing, 'brought off a good deal besides furs.' Then he went back — heavens, how far ! — to ask about the *Chesapeake*, and what was done to Barron for surrendering her to the *Leopard*, and whether Burr ever tried again; and he ground his teeth with the only passion he showed. But in a moment that was over, 10 and he said, 'God forgive me, for I am sure I forgive him.' Then he asked about the old war — told me the true story of his serving the gun the day we took the *Java;* asked about dear old David Porter, as he called him. Then he settled down more quietly, and very happily, to hear me tell in an hour the history 15 of fifty years.

"How I wished it had been somebody who knew something ! But I did as well as I could. I told him of the English war. I told him about Fulton and the steamboat beginning. I told him about old Scott, and Jackson; told him all I could think of 20 about the Mississippi, and New Orleans, and Texas, and his own old Kentucky. And do you think, he asked who was in command of the 'Legion of the West.' I told him it was a very gallant officer named Grant, and that, by our last news, he was about to establish his headquarters at Vicksburg. Then, 25 'Where was Vicksburg?' I worked that out on the map; it was about a hundred miles, more or less, above his old Fort Adams; and I thought Fort Adams must be a ruin now. 'It must be at old Vick's plantation, at Walnut Hills,' said he: 'well, that is a change !' 30

"I tell you, Ingham, it was a hard thing to condense the history of half a century into that talk with a sick man. And I do not now know what I told him — of emigration, and the means of it — of steamboats, and railroads, and telegraphs, of inventions, and books, and literature — of the colleges, and West

28   SELECTIONS FOR THE EIGHTH GRADE

Point, and the Naval School — but with the queerest interruptions that you ever heard.   You see it was Robinson Crusoe asking all the accumulated questions of fifty-six years !

"I remember he asked, all of a sudden, who was President now;
5 and when I told him, he asked if Old Abe was General Benjamin Lincoln's son.   He said he met old General Lincoln, when he was quite a boy himself, at some Indian treaty.   I said no, that Old Abe was a Kentuckian like himself, but I could not tell him of what family; he had worked up from the ranks. 'Good for
10 him !' cried Nolan; 'I am glad of that.   As I have brooded and wondered, I have thought our danger was in keeping up those regular successions in the first families.'   Then I got talking about my visit to Washington.   I told him of meeting the Oregon Congressman, Harding; I told him about the Smithsonian, and
15 the Exploring Expedition; I told him about the Capitol, and the statues for the pediment, and Crawford's Liberty, and Greenough's Washington; Ingham, I told him everything I could think of that would show the grandeur of his country and its prosperity; but I could not make up my mouth to
20 tell him a word about this infernal rebellion !

"And he drank it in and enjoyed it as I cannot tell you.   He grew more and more silent, yet I never thought he was tired or faint.   I gave him a glass of water, but he just wet his lips, and told me not to go away.   Then he asked me to bring the Pres-
25 byterian 'Book of Public Prayer' which lay there, and said, with a smile, that it would open at the right place — and so it did. There was his double red mark down the page; and I knelt down and read, and he repeated with me, 'For ourselves and our country, O gracious God, we thank Thee, that, notwithstanding
30 our manifold transgressions of Thy holy laws, Thou hast continued to us Thy marvelous kindness' — and so to the end of that thanksgiving.   Then he turned to the end of the same book, and I read the words more familiar to me : 'Most heartily we beseech Thee with Thy favor to behold and bless Thy servant, the President of the United States, and all others in

THE MAN WITHOUT A COUNTRY 29

authority ' — and the rest of the Episcopal collect. 'Danforth,' said he, 'I have repeated those prayers night and morning, it is now fifty-five years.' And then he said he would go to sleep. He bent me down over him and kissed me; and he said, 'Look in my Bible, Danforth, when I am gone.' And I went away. 5

"But I had no thought it was the end. I thought he was tired and would sleep. I knew he was happy, and I wanted him to be alone.

"But in an hour, when the doctor went in gently, he found Nolan had breathed his life away with a smile. He had some- 10 thing pressed closed to his lips. It was his father's badge of the Order of the Cincinnati.

"We looked in his Bible, and there was a slip of paper at the place where he had marked the text:

"'They desire a country, even a heavenly: wherefore God is 15 not ashamed to be called their God: for He hath prepared for them a city.'

"On this slip of paper he had written: —

"'Bury me in the sea; it has been my home, and I love it. But will not some one set up a stone for my memory at Fort 20 Adams or at Orleans, that my disgrace may not be more than I ought to bear? Say on it: —

"'*In Memory of*

"'PHILIP NOLAN,

"'*Lieutenant in the Army of the United States.* 25

"'He loved his country as no other man has loved her; but no man deserved less at her hands.'"

SELECTIONS FOR THE EIGHTH GRADE

THE SKELETON IN ARMOR

HENRY WADSWORTH LONGFELLOW

NOTE. Longfellow says in his notes: "This ballad was suggested to me while riding on the seashore at Newport. A skeleton clad in broken armor had been dug up at Fall River and the idea occurred to me of connecting it with the Round Tower at Newport, generally known as the Old Windmill, though now claimed by the Danes as the work of their early ancestors."

"Speak! speak! thou fearful guest!
Who, with thy hollow breast
Still in rude armor drest
  Comest to daunt me!
Wrapt not in Eastern balms,
But with thy fleshless palms
Stretched, as if asking alms,
  Why dost thou haunt me?"

Then from those cavernous eyes
Pale flashes seemed to rise,
As when the Northern skies
  Gleam in December;
And, like the water's flow
Under December's snow,
Came a dull voice of woe
  From the heart's chamber.

"I was a Viking old!
My deeds, though manifold,
No Skald in song has told,
  No Saga taught thee!
Take heed that in thy verse
Thou dost the tale rehearse,
Else dread a dead man's curse;
  For this I sought thee.

THE SKELETON IN ARMOR

"Far in the Northern Land,
By the wild Baltic's strand,
I, with my childish hand,
  Tamed the gerfalcon;
And, with my skates fast-bound,
Skimmed the half-frozen Sound,
That the poor whimpering hound
  Trembled to walk on.

"Oft to his frozen lair
Tracked I the grisly bear,   10
While from my path the hare
  Fled like a shadow;
Oft through the forest dark
Followed the werewolf's bark,
Until the soaring lark   15
  Sang from the meadow.

"But when I older grew,
Joining a corsair's crew,
O'er the dark sea I flew
  With the marauders.   20
Wild was the life we led;
Many the souls that sped,
Many the hearts that bled,
  By our stern orders.

"Many a wassail-bout   25
Wore the long Winter out;
Often our midnight shout
  Set the cocks crowing,
As we the Berserk's tale
Measured in cups of ale,   30
Draining the oaken pail
  Filled to o'erflowing.

SELECTIONS FOR THE EIGHTH GRADE

"Once as I told in glee
Tales of the stormy sea,
Soft eyes did gaze on me,
     Burning yet tender;
And as the white stars shine
On the dark Norway pine,
On that dark heart of mine
     Fell their soft splendor.

"I wooed the blue-eyed maid,
Yielding, yet half afraid,
And in the forest's shade
     Our vows were plighted.
Under its loosened vest
Fluttered her little breast,
Like birds within their nest
     By the hawk frighted.

"Bright in her father's hall
Shields gleamed upon the wall,
Loud sang the minstrels all,
     Chanting his glory;
When of old Hildebrand
I asked his daughter's hand,
Mute did the minstrels stand
     To hear my story.

"While the brown ale he quaffed,
Loud then the champion laughed,
And as the wind-gusts waft
     The sea-foam brightly,
So the loud laugh of scorn,
Out of those lips unshorn,
From the deep drinking-horn
     Blew the foam lightly.

THE SKELETON IN ARMOR

"She was a Prince's child,
I but a Viking wild,
And though she blushed and smiled,
  I was discarded!
Should not the dove so white
Follow the sea-mew's flight?
Why did they leave that night
  Her nest unguarded?

"Scarce had I put to sea,
Bearing the maid with me, —   10
Fairest of all was she
  Among the Norsemen! —
When on the white sea-strand,
Waving his armèd hand,
Saw we old Hildebrand,   15
  With twenty horsemen.

"Then launched they to the blast,
Bent like a reed each mast,
Yet we were gaining fast,
  When the wind failed us;   20
And with a sudden flaw
Came round the gusty Skaw,
So that our foe we saw
  Laugh as he hailed us.

"And as to catch the gale   25
Round veered the flapping sail,
'Death!' was the helmsman's hail,
  'Death without quarter!'
Midships with iron keel
Struck we her ribs of steel;   30
Down her black hulk did reel
  Through the black water!

34   SELECTIONS FOR THE EIGHTH GRADE

"As with his wings aslant,
Sails the fierce cormorant,
Seeking some rocky haunt,
    With his prey laden,
So toward the open main,
Beating to sea again,
Through the wild hurricane,
    Bore I the maiden.

"Three weeks we westward bore,
And when the storm was o'er,
Cloud-like we saw the shore
    Stretching to leeward;
There for my lady's bower
Built I the lofty tower,
Which, to this very hour,
    Stands looking seaward.

"There lived we many years;
Time dried the maiden's tears;
She had forgot her fears,
    She was a mother;
Death closed her mild blue eyes;
Under that tower she lies;
Ne'er shall the sun arise
    On such another.

"Still grew my bosom then,
Still as a stagnant fen!
Hateful to me were men,
    The sunlight hateful!
In the vast forest here,
Clad in my warlike gear,
Fell I upon my spear,
    Oh, death was grateful!

HORATIUS

35

"Thus, seamed with many scars,
Bursting these prison bars,
Up to its native stars
   My soul ascended !
There from the flowing bowl
Deep drinks the warrior's soul,
Skoal ! to the Northland ! *skoal !*"
Thus the tale ended.

HORATIUS

A LAY MADE ABOUT THE YEAR OF THE CITY CCCLX

THOMAS BABINGTON MACAULAY

NOTE. "There can be little doubt that among those parts of early
Roman history which had a poetical origin was the legend of Horatius
Cocles. We have several versions of the story, and these versions differ from
each other in points of no small importance. According to Polybius, Hora-
tius defended the bridge alone, and perished in the waters. According to
the chronicles which Livy and Dionysius followed, Horatius had two com-
panions, swam safe to shore, and was loaded with honors and rewards. . . .
It is by no means unlikely that there were two old Roman lays about the
defense of the bridge ; and that, while the story which Livy has transmitted
to us was preferred by the multitude, the other, which ascribed the whole
glory to Horatius alone, may have been the favorite with the Horatian house.
   The following ballad is supposed to have been made about a hundred and
twenty years after the war which it celebrates, and just before the taking of
Rome by the Gauls. The author seems to have been an honest citizen,
proud of the military glory of his country, sick of the disputes of factions,
and much given to pining after good old times which had never really
existed."   T. B. M.

I

Lars Porsena of Clusium
   By the Nine Gods he swore   10
That the great house of Tarquin
   Should suffer wrong no more.
By the Nine Gods he swore it,

SELECTIONS FOR THE EIGHTH GRADE

And named a trysting day,
And bade his messengers ride forth,
East and west and south and north,
To summon his array.

II

East and west and south and north
The messengers ride fast,
And tower and town and cottage
Have heard the trumpet's blast.
Shame on the false Etruscan
Who lingers in his home,
When Porsena of Clusium
Is on the march for Rome.

III

The horsemen and the footmen
Are pouring in amain
From many a stately marketplace;
From many a fruitful plain;
From many a lonely hamlet,
Which, hid by beech and pine,
Like an eagle's nest, hangs on the crest
Of purple Apennine;

IV

From lordly Volaterræ,
Where scowls the far-famed hold
Piled by the hands of giants
For godlike kings of old;
From seagirt Populonia,
Whose sentinels descry
Sardinia's snowy mountain tops
Fringing the southern sky;

HORATIUS

V

From the proud mart of Pisæ,
  Queen of the western waves,
Where ride Massilia's triremes
  Heavy with fair-haired slaves;
From where sweet Clanis wanders
  Through corn and vines and flowers;
From where Cortona lifts to heaven
  Her diadem of towers.

VI

Tall are the oaks whose acorns
  Drop in dark Auser's rill;
Fat are the stags that champ the boughs
  Of the Ciminian hill;
Beyond all streams Clitumnus
  Is to the herdsman dear;
Best of all pools the fowler loves
  The great Volsinian mere.

VII

But now no stroke of woodman
  Is heard by Auser's rill;
No hunter tracks the stag's green path
  Up the Ciminian hill;
Unwatched along Clitumnus
  Grazes the milk-white steer;
Unharmed the water fowl may dip
  In the Volsinian mere.

VIII

The harvests of Arretium,
  This year, old men shall reap;
This year, young boys in Umbro
  Shall plunge the struggling sheep;

SELECTIONS FOR THE EIGHTH GRADE

And in the vats of Luna,
This year, the must shall foam
Round the white feet of laughing girls
Whose sires have marched to Rome.

IX

There be thirty chosen prophets,
The wisest of the land,
Who alway by Lars Porsena
Both morn and evening stand:
Evening and morn the Thirty
Have turned the verses o'er,
Traced from the right on linen white
By mighty seers of yore.

X

And with one voice the Thirty
Have their glad answer given:
"Go forth, go forth, Lars Porsena;
Go forth, beloved of Heaven;
Go, and return in glory
To Clusium's royal dome;
And hang round Nurscia's altars
The golden shields of Rome."

XI

And now hath every city
Sent up her tale of men;
The foot are fourscore thousand,
The horse are thousands ten.
Before the gates of Sutrium
Is met the great array.
A proud man was Lars Porsena
Upon the trysting day.

HORATIUS

XII

For all the Etruscan armies
  Were ranged beneath his eye,
And many a banished Roman,
  And many a stout ally;
And with a mighty following
  To join the muster came
The Tusculan Mamilius,
  Prince of the Latian name.

XIII

But by the yellow Tiber
  Was tumult and affright: 10
From all the spacious champaign
  To Rome men took their flight.
A mile around the city,
  The throng stopped up the ways;
A fearful sight it was to see   15
  Through two long nights and days.

XIV

For aged folk on crutches,
  And women great with child,
And mothers sobbing over babes
  That clung to them and smiled,   20
And sick men borne in litters
  High on the necks of slaves,
And troops of sunburned husbandmen
  With reaping-hooks and staves,

XV

And droves of mules and asses   25
  Laden with skins of wine,
And endless flocks of goats and sheep,
  And endless herds of kine,

40 SELECTIONS FOR THE EIGHTH GRADE

And endless trains of wagons
  That creaked beneath the weight
Of corn sacks and of household goods,
  Choked every roaring gate.

XVI

Now, from the rock Tarpeian,
  Could the wan burghers spy
The line of blazing villages
  Red in the midnight sky.
The Fathers of the City,
  They sat all night and day,
For every hour some horseman came
  With tidings of dismay.

XVII

To eastward and to westward
  Have spread the Tuscan bands;
Nor house, nor fence, nor dovecote
  In Crustumerium stands.
Verbenna down to Ostia
  Hath wasted all the plain;
Astur hath stormed Janiculum,
  And the stout guards are slain.

XVIII

I wis, in all the Senate,
  There was no heart so bold,
But sore it ached, and fast it beat,
  When that ill news was told.
Forthwith up rose the Consul,
  Up rose the Fathers all;
In haste they girded up their gowns,
  And hied them to the wall.

HORATIUS

XIX

They held a council standing
  Before the River-Gate;
Short time was there, ye well may guess,
  For musing or debate.
Out spake the Consul roundly: 5
  "The bridge must straight go down;
For, since Janiculum is lost,
  Nought else can save the town."

XX

Just then a scout came flying,
  All wild with haste and fear: 10
"To arms ! to arms ! Sir Consul:
  Lars Porsena is here."
On the low hills to westward
  The Consul fixed his eye,
And saw the swarthy storm of dust   15
  Rise fast along the sky.

XXI

And nearer fast and nearer
  Doth the red whirlwind come;
And louder still and still more loud,
From underneath that rolling cloud,   20
Is heard the trumpet's war note proud,
  The trampling, and the hum.
And plainly and more plainly
  Now through the gloom appears,
Far to left and far to right,   25
In broken gleams of dark-blue light,
The long array of helmets bright,
  The long array of spears.

SELECTIONS FOR THE EIGHTH GRADE

XXII

And plainly and more plainly,
　Above that glimmering line,
Now might ye see the banners
　Of twelve fair cities shine;
But the banner of proud Clusium
　Was highest of them all,
The terror of the Umbrian,
　The terror of the Gaul.

XXIII

And plainly and more plainly
　Now might the burghers know,
By port and vest, by horse and crest,
　Each warlike Lucumo.
There Cilnius of Arretium
　On his fleet roan was seen
And Astur of the fourfold shield,
Girt with the brand none else may wield,
Tolumnius with the belt of gold,
And dark Verbenna from the hold
　By reedy Thrasymene.

XXIV

Fast by the royal standard,
　O'erlooking all the war,
Lars Porsena of Clusium
　Sat in his ivory car.
By the right wheel rode Mamilius,
　Prince of the Latian name;
And by the left false Sextus,
　That wrought the deed of shame.

HORATIUS

43

XXV

But when the face of Sextus
    Was seen among the foes,
A yell that rent the firmament
    From all the town arose.
On the housetops was no woman   5
    But spat towards him and hissed,
No child but screamed out curses,
    And shook its little fist.

XXVI

But the Consul's brow was sad,
    And the Consul's speech was low,   10
And darkly looked he at the wall,
    And darkly at the foe.
"Their van will be upon us
    Before the bridge goes down;
And if they once may win the bridge,   15
    What hope to save the town?"

XXVII

Then out spake brave Horatius,
    The Captain of the Gate:
"To every man upon this earth
    Death ‚cometh soon or late.   20
And how can man die better
    Than facing fearful odds,
For the ashes of his fathers,
    And the temples of his Gods,

XXVIII

"And for the tender mother   25
    Who dandled him to rest,
And for the wife who nurses
    His baby at her breast,

SELECTIONS FOR THE EIGHTH GRADE

And for the holy maidens
  Who feed the eternal flame,
To save them from false Sextus
  That wrought the deed of shame?

XXIX

"Hew down the bridge, Sir Consul,
  With all the speed ye may;
I, with two more to help me,
  Will hold the foe in play.
In yon strait path a thousand
  May well be stopped by three.
Now who will stand on either hand,
  And keep the bridge with me?"

XXX

Then out spake Spurius Lartius;
  A Ramnian proud was he:
"Lo, I will stand at thy right hand,
  And keep the bridge with thee."
And out spake strong Herminius;
  Of Titian blood was he:
"I will abide on thy left side,
  And keep the bridge with thee."

XXXI

"Horatius," quoth the Consul,
  "As thou sayest, so let it be."
And straight against that great array
  Forth went the dauntless Three.
For Romans in Rome's quarrel
  Spared neither land nor gold,
Nor son nor wife, nor limb nor life,
  In the brave days of old.

HORATIUS

XXXII

Then none was for a party;
  Then all were for the state;
Then the great man helped the poor,
  And the poor man loved the great:
Then lands were fairly portioned;
  Then spoils were fairly sold:
The Romans were like brothers
  In the brave days of old.

XXXIII

Now Roman is to Roman
  More hateful than a foe,
And the Tribunes beard the high,
  And the Fathers grind the low.
As we wax hot in faction,
  In battle we wax cold:
Wherefore men fight not as they fought
  In the brave days of old.

XXXIV

Now while the Three were tightening
  Their harness on their backs,
The Consul was the foremost man
  To take in hand an ax:
And Fathers mixed with Commons
  Seized hatchet, bar, and crow,
And smote upon the planks above,
  And loosed the props below.

XXXV

Meanwhile the Tuscan army,
  Right glorious to behold,

46 SELECTIONS FOR THE EIGHTH GRADE

Came flashing back the noonday light,
Rank behind rank, like surges bright
  Of a broad sea of gold.
Four hundred trumpets sounded
  A peal of warlike glee,
As that great host, with measured tread,
And spears advanced, and ensigns spread,
Rolled slowly towards the bridge's head,
  Where stood the dauntless Three.

XXXVI

10   The Three stood calm and silent,
  And looked upon the foes,
And a great shout of laughter
  From all the vanguard rose:
And forth three chiefs came spurring
15   Before that deep array;
To earth they sprang, their swords they drew,
And lifted high their shields, and flew
  To win the narrow way;

XXXVII

Aunus from green Tifernum,
20   Lord of the Hill of Vines;
And Seius, whose eight hundred slaves
  Sicken in Ilva's mines;
And Picus, long to Clusium
  Vassal in peace and war,
25   Who led to fight his Umbrian powers
From that gray crag where, girt with towers,
The fortress of Nequinum lowers
  O'er the pale waves of Nar.

HORATIUS

XXXVIII

Stout Lartius hurled down Aunus
  Into the stream beneath:
Herminius struck at Seius,
  And clove him to the teeth:
At Picus brave Horatius
  Darted one fiery thrust;
And the proud Umbrian's gilded arms
  Clashed in the bloody dust.

XXXIX

Then Ocnus of Falerii
  Rushed on the Roman Three;
And Lausulus of Urgo,
  The rover of the sea;
And Aruns of Volsinium,
  Who slew the great wild boar,
The great wild boar that had his den
Amidst the reeds of Cosa's fen,
And wasted fields, and slaughtered men,
  Along Albinia's shore.

XL

Herminius smote down Aruns:
  Lartius laid Ocnus low:
Right to the heart of Lausulus
  Horatius sent a blow.
"Lie there," he cried, "fell pirate!
  No more, aghast and pale,
From Ostia's walls the crowd shall mark
The track of thy destroying bark.
No more Campania's hinds shall fly
To woods and caverns when they spy
  Thy thrice accursed sail."

SELECTIONS FOR THE EIGHTH GRADE

XLI

But now no sound of laughter
Was heard among the foes.
A wild and wrathful clamor
From all the vanguard rose.
Six spears' lengths from the entrance
Halted that deep array,
And for a space no man came forth
To win the narrow way.

XLII

But hark! the cry is Astur:
And lo! the ranks divide;
And the great Lord of Luna
Comes with his stately stride.
Upon his ample shoulders
Clangs loud the fourfold shield,
And in his hand he shakes the brand
Which none but he can wield.

XLIII

He smiled on those bold Romans
A smile serene and high;
He eyed the flinching Tuscans,
And scorn was in his eye.
Quoth he, "The she-wolf's litter
Stand savagely at bay:
But will ye dare to follow,
If Astur clears the way?"

XLIV

Then, whirling up his broadsword
With both hands to the height,
He rushed against Horatius,
And smote with all his might.

HORATIUS

With shield and blade Horatius
  Right deftly turned the blow.
The blow, though turned, came yet too nigh;
It missed his helm, but gashed his thigh:
The Tuscans raised a joyful cry
  To see the red blood flow.

XLV

He reeled, and on Herminius
  He leaned one breathing-space;
Then, like a wildcat mad with wounds,
  Sprang right at Astur's face.   10
Through teeth, and skull, and helmet
  So fierce a thrust he sped,
The good sword stood a handbreadth out
  Behind the Tuscan's head.

XLVI

And the great Lord of Luna   15
  Fell at that deadly stroke,
As falls on Mount Alvernus
  A thunder-smitten oak.
Far o'er the crashing forest
  The giant arms lie spread;   20
And the pale augurs, muttering low,
  Gaze on the blasted head.

XLVII

On Astur's throat Horatius
  Right firmly pressed his heel,
And thrice and four times tugged amain,   25
  Ere he wrenched out the steel.
"And see," he cried, "the welcome,
  Fair guests, that waits you here!
What noble Lucumo comes next
  To taste our Roman cheer?"

SELECTIONS FOR THE EIGHTH GRADE

XLVIII

But at his haughty challenge
  A sullen murmur ran,
Mingled of wrath, and shame, and dread,
  Along that glittering van.
There lacked not men of prowess,
  Nor men of lordly race;
For all Etruria's noblest
  Were round the fatal place.

XLIX

But all Etruria's noblest
  Felt their hearts sink to see
On the earth the bloody corpses,
  In the path the dauntless Three:
And, from the ghastly entrance
  Where those bold Romans stood,
All shrank, like boys who unaware,
Ranging the woods to start a hare,
Come to the mouth of the dark lair
Where, growling low, a fierce old bear
  Lies amidst bones and blood.

L

Was none who would be foremost
  To lead such dire attack:
But those behind cried "Forward!"
  And those before cried "Back!"
And backward now and forward
  Wavers the deep array;
And on the tossing sea of steel,
To and fro the standards reel;
And the victorious trumpet-peal
  Dies fitfully away.

HORATIUS

51

LI

Yet one man for one moment
  Strode out before the crowd;
Well known was he to all the Three,
  And they gave him greeting loud.
"Now welcome, welcome, Sextus!   5
  Now welcome to thy home!
Why dost thou stay, and turn away?
  Here lies the road to Rome."

LII

Thrice looked he at the city;
  Thrice looked he at the dead;   10
And thrice came on in fury,
  And thrice turned back in dread:
And, white with fear and hatred,
  Scowled at the narrow way
Where, wallowing in a pool of blood,   15
  The bravest Tuscans lay.

LIII

But meanwhile ax and lever
  Have manfully been plied;
And now the bridge hangs tottering
  Above the boiling tide.   20
"Come back, come back, Horatius!"
  Loud cried the Fathers all.
"Back, Lartius! back, Herminius!
  Back, ere the ruin fall!"

LIV

Back darted Spurius Lartius;   25
  Herminius darted back:
And, as they passed, beneath their feet
  They felt the timbers crack.

52   SELECTIONS FOR THE EIGHTH GRADE

But when they turned their faces,
  And on the farther shore
Saw brave Horatius stand alone,
  They would have crossed once more.

LV •

But with a crash like thunder
  Fell every loosened beam,
And, like a dam, the mighty wreck
  Lay right athwart the stream:
And a long shout of triumph
10   Rose from the walls of Rome,
As to the highest turret tops
  Was splashed the yellow foam.

LVI

And, like a horse unbroken
  When first he feels the rein,
15 The furious river struggled hard,
  And tossed his tawny mane,
And burst the curb, and bounded,
  Rejoicing to be free,
And whirling down, in fierce career,
20 Battlement, and plank, and pier,
  Rushed headlong to the sea.

LVII

Alone stood brave Horatius,
  But constant still in mind;
Thrice thirty thousand foes before,
25   And the broad flood behind.
"Down with him!" cried false Sextus,
  With a smile on his pale face.
"Now yield thee," cried Lars Porsena,
  "Now yield thee to our grace."

HORATIUS

53

LVIII

Round turned he, as not deigning
  Those craven ranks to see;
Nought spake he to Lars Porsena,
  To Sextus nought spake he;
But he saw on Palatinus
  The white porch of his home;
And he spake to the noble river
  That rolls by the towers of Rome.

LIX

"O Tiber! father Tiber!
  To whom the Romans pray,   10
A Roman's life, a Roman's arms,
  Take thou in charge this day!"
So he spake, and speaking sheathed
  The good sword by his side,
And with his harness on his back,   15
  Plunged headlong in the tide.

LX

No sound of joy or sorrow
  Was heard from either bank;
But friends and foes in dumb surprise,
With parted lips and straining eyes,   20
  Stood gazing where he sank;
And when above the surges
  They saw his crest appear,
All Rome sent forth a rapturous cry,
And even the ranks of Tuscany   25
  Could scarce forbear to cheer.

SELECTIONS FOR THE EIGHTH GRADE

LXI

But fiercely ran the current,
  Swollen high by months of rain:
And fast his blood was flowing;
  And he was sore in pain,
And heavy with his armor,
  And spent with changing blows:
And oft they thought him sinking,
  But still again he rose.

LXII

Never, I ween, did swimmer,
  In such an evil case,
Struggle through such a raging flood
  Safe to the landing place:
But his limbs were borne up bravely
  By the brave heart within,
And our good father Tiber
  Bare bravely up his chin.

LXIII

"Curse on him!" quoth false Sextus;
  "Will not the villain drown?
But for this stay, ere close of day
  We should have sacked the town!"
"Heaven help him!" quoth Lars Porsena,
  "And bring him safe to shore;
For such a gallant feat of arms
  Was never seen before."

LXIV

And now he feels the bottom;
  Now on dry earth he stands;
Now round him throng the Fathers
  To press his gory hands;

HORATIUS

And now, with shouts and clapping,
   And noise of weeping loud,
He enters through the River-Gate,
   Borne by the joyous crowd.

LXV

They gave him of the corn-land,
   That was of public right,
As much as two strong oxen
   Could plow from morn till night;
And they made a molten image,
   And set it up on high,   10
And there it stands unto this day
   To witness if I lie.

LXVI

It stands in the Comitium,
   Plain for all folk to see;
Horatius in his harness,   15
   Halting upon one knee:
And underneath is written,
   In letters all of gold,
How valiantly he kept the bridge
   In the brave days of old.   20

LXVII

And still his name sounds stirring
   Unto the men of Rome,
As the trumpet-blast that cries to them
   To charge the Volscian home;
And wives still pray to Juno   25
   For boys with hearts as bold
As his who kept the bridge so well
   In the brave days of old.

56 SELECTIONS FOR THE EIGHTH GRADE

LXVIII

And in the nights of winter,
  When the cold north winds blow,
And the long howling of the wolves
  Is heard amidst the snow;
When round the lonely cottage
  Roars loud the tempest's din,
And the good logs of Algidus
  Roar louder yet within;

LXIX

When the oldest cask is opened,
  And the largest lamp is lit;
When the chestnuts glow in the embers,
  And the kid turns on the spit;
When young and old in circle
  Around the firebrands close;
When the girls are weaving baskets,
  And the lads are shaping bows;

LXX

When the goodman mends his armor,
  And trims his helmet's plume;
When the goodwife's shuttle merrily
  Goes flashing through the loom;
With weeping and with laughter
  Still is the story told,
How well Horatius kept the bridge
  In the brave days of old.

THE SINGING LEAVES

A BALLAD

James Russell Lowell

1

"What fairings will ye that I bring?"
  Said the King to his daughters three;
"For I to Vanity Fair am boun,
  Now say what shall they be?"

Then up and spake the eldest daughter,
  That lady tall and grand:
"O, bring me pearls and diamonds great,
  And gold rings for my hand."

Thereafter spake the second daughter,
  That was both white and red: 10
"For me bring silks that will stand alone,
  And a gold comb for my head."

Then came the turn of the least daughter,
  That was whiter than thistledown,
And among the gold of her blithesome hair   15
  Dim shone the golden crown.

"There came a bird this morning,
  And sang 'neath my bower eaves,
Till I dreamed, as his music made me,
  'Ask thou for the Singing Leaves.'"   20

Then the brow of the King swelled crimson
  With a flush of angry scorn:
"Well have ye spoken, my two eldest,
  And chosen as ye were born;

58 SELECTIONS FOR THE EIGHTH GRADE

"But she, like a thing of peasant race,
    That is happy binding the sheaves," —
Then he saw her dead mother in her face,
    And said, "Thou shalt have thy leaves."

II

He mounted and rode three days and nights
    Till he came to Vanity Fair,
And 'twas easy to buy the gems and the silk,
    But no Singing Leaves were there.

Then deep in the greenwood rode he,
10   And asked of every tree,
"O, if you have ever a Singing Leaf,
    I pray you give it me!"

But the trees all kept their counsel,
    And never a word said they,
15 Only there sighed from the pine tops
    A music of seas far away.

Only the pattering aspen
    Made a sound of growing rain,
That fell ever faster and faster,
20   Then faltered to silence again.

"O, where shall I find a little foot-page
    That would win both hose and shoon,
And will bring to me the Singing Leaves
    If they grow under the moon?"

25 Then lightly turned him Walter the page,
    By the stirrup as he ran:
"Now pledge you me the truesome word
    Of a king and gentleman,

THE SINGING LEAVES 59

"That you will give me the first, first thing
    You meet at your castle gate,
And the Princess shall get the Singing Leaves,
    Or mine be a traitor's fate."

The King's head dropt upon his breast
    A moment, as it might be;
'Twill be my dog; he thought, and said,
    "My faith I plight to thee."

Then Walter took from next his heart
    A packet small and thin,   10
"Now give you this to the Princess Anne,
    The Singing Leaves are therein."

III

As the King rode in at his castle gate,
    A maiden to meet him ran,
And "Welcome, father!" she laughed and cried   15
    Together, the Princess Anne.

"Lo, here the Singing Leaves," quoth he,
    "And woe, but they cost me dear!"
She took the packet, and the smile
    Deepened down beneath the tear.   20

It deepened down till it reached her heart,
    And then gushed up again,
And lighted her tears as the sudden sun
    Transfigures the summer rain.

And the first Leaf, when it was opened,   25
    Sang: "I am Walter the page,
And the songs I sing 'neath thy window
    Are my only heritage."

SELECTIONS FOR THE EIGHTH GRADE

And the second Leaf sang: "But in the land
    That is neither on earth or sea,
My lute and I are lords of more
    Than thrice this kingdom's fee."

And the third Leaf sang, "Be mine ! Be mine !"
    And ever it sang, "Be mine !"
Then sweeter it sang and ever sweeter,
    And said, "I am thine, thine, thine !"

At the first Leaf she grew pale enough,
    At the second she turned aside,
At the third, 'twas as if a lily flushed
    With a rose's red heart's tide.

"Good counsel gave the bird," said she,
    "I have my hope thrice o'er,
For they sing to my very heart," she said,
    "And it sings to them evermore."

She brought to him her beauty and truth,
    But and broad earldoms three,
And he made her queen of the broader lands
    He held of his lute in fee.

RHŒCUS

James Russell Lowell

God sends his teachers unto every age,
To every clime, and every race of men,
With revelations fitted to their growth
And shape of mind, nor gives the realm of Truth
Into the selfish rule of one sole race:

RHŒCUS

Therefore each form of worship that hath swayed
The life of man, and given it to grasp
The master-key of knowledge, reverence,
Enfolds some germs of goodness and of right;
Else never had the eager soul, which loathes   5
The slothful down of pampered ignorance,
Found in it even a moment's fitful rest.

There is an instinct in the human heart
Which makes that all the fables it hath coined,
To justify the reign of its belief   10
And strengthen it by beauty's right divine,
Veil in their inner cells a mystic gift,
Which, like the hazel twig, in faithful hands,
Points surely to the hidden springs of truth.
For, as in nature nought is made in vain,   15
But all things have within their hull of use
A wisdom and a meaning which may speak
Of spiritual secrets to the ear
Of spirit; so, in whatsoe'er the heart
Hath fashioned for a solace to itself,   20
To make its inspirations suit its creed,
And from the niggard hands of falsehood wring
Its needful food of truth, there ever is
A sympathy with Nature, which reveals,
Not less than her own works, pure gleams of light   25
And earnest parables of inward lore.
Hear now this fairy legend of old Greece,
As full of gracious youth, and beauty still
As the immortal freshness of that grace
Carved for all ages on some Attic frieze.   30

A youth named Rhœcus, wandering in the wood,
Saw an old oak just trembling to its fall,
And, feeling pity of so fair a tree,
He propped its gray trunk with admiring care,

SELECTIONS FOR THE EIGHTH GRADE

And with a thoughtless footstep loitered on.
But, as he turned, he heard a voice behind
That murmured " Rhœcus ! "   'Twas as if the leaves,
Stirred by a passing breath, had murmured it,
And, while he paused bewildered, yet again
It murmured " Rhœcus ! " softer than a breeze.
He started, and beheld with dizzy eyes
What seemed the substance of a happy dream
Stand there before him, spreading a warm glow
10 Within the green glooms of the shadowy oak.
It seemed a woman's shape, yet far too fair
To be a woman, and with eyes too meek
For any that were wont to mate with gods.
All naked like a goddess stood she there,
15 And like a goddess all too beautiful
To feel the guilt-born earthliness of shame.
" Rhœcus, I am the Dryad of this tree,"
Thus she began, dropping her low-toned words
Serene, and full, and clear, as drops of dew,
20 " And with it I am doomed to live and die ;
The rain and sunshine are my caterers,
Nor have I other bliss than simple life ;
Now ask me what thou wilt, that I can give,
And with a thankful joy it shall be thine."

25   Then Rhœcus, with a flutter at the heart,
Yet, by the prompting of such beauty, bold,
Answered : " What is there that can satisfy
The endless craving of the soul but love ?
Give me thy love, or but the hope of that
30 Which must be evermore my nature's goal."
After a little pause she said again,
But with a glimpse of sadness in her tone,
" I give it, Rhœcus, though a perilous gift ;
An hour before the sunset meet me here."

RHŒCUS

And straightway there was nothing he could see
But the green glooms beneath the shadowy oak,
And not a sound came to his straining ears
But the low trickling rustle of the leaves,
And far away upon an emerald slope
The falter of an idle shepherd's pipe.

Now, in those days of simpleness and faith,
Men did not think that happy things were dreams
Because they overstepped the narrow bourn
Of likelihood, but reverently deemed   10
Nothing too wondrous or too beautiful
To be the guerdon of a daring heart.
So Rhœcus made no doubt that he was blest,
And all along unto the city's gate
Earth seemed to spring beneath him as he walked,   15
The clear, broad sky looked bluer than its wont,
And he could scarce believe he had not wings,
Such sunshine seemed to glitter through his veins
Instead of blood, so light he felt and strange.

Young Rhœcus had a faithful heart enough,   20
But one that in the present dwelt too much,
And, taking with blithe welcome whatsoe'er
Chance gave of joy, was wholly bound in that,
Like the contented peasant of a vale,
Deemed it the world, and never looked beyond.   25
So, haply meeting in the afternoon
Some comrades who were playing at the dice,
He joined them, and forgot all else beside.

The dice were rattling at the merriest,
And Rhœcus, who had met but sorry luck,   30
Just laughed in triumph at a happy throw,
When through the room there hummed a yellow bee
That buzzed about his ear with down-dropped legs

64 SELECTIONS FOR THE EIGHTH GRADE

As if to light.   And Rhœcus laughed and said,
Feeling how red and flushed he was with loss,
" By Venus ! does he take me for a rose ? "
And brushed him off with rough, impatient hand.
But still the bee came back, and thrice again
Rhœcus did beat him off with growing wrath.
Then through the window flew the wounded bee,
And Rhœcus tracking him with angry eyes,
Saw a sharp mountain peak of Thessaly
10   Against the red disk of the setting sun, —
And instantly the blood sank from his heart,
As if its very walls had caved away.
Without a word he turned, and, rushing forth,
Ran madly through the city and the gate,
15   And o'er the plain, which now the wood's long shade,
By the low sun thrown forward broad and dim,
Darkened wellnigh unto the city's wall.

Quite spent and out of breath he reached the tree,
And, listening fearfully, he heard once more
20   The low voice murmur " Rhœcus ! " close at hand :
Whereat he looked around him, but could see
Nought but the deepening glooms beneath the oak.
Then sighed the voice, " O Rhœcus ! nevermore
Shalt thou behold me or by day or night,
25   Me, who would fain have blessed thee with a love
More ripe and bounteous than ever yet
Filled up with nectar any mortal heart :
But thou didst scorn my humble messenger,
And sent'st him back to me with bruisèd wings.
30   We spirits only show to gentle eyes ;
We ever ask an undivided love ;
And he who scorns the least of Nature's works
Is thenceforth exiled and shut out from all.
Farewell ! for thou canst never see me more."

WASHINGTON

Then Rhœcus beat his breast, and groaned aloud,
And cried, "Be pitiful! forgive me yet
This once, and I shall never need it more!"
"Alas!" the voice returned, "'tis thou art blind,
Not I unmerciful; I can forgive,
But have no skill to heal thy spirit's eyes;
Only the soul hath power o'er itself."
With that again there murmured "Nevermore!"
And Rhœcus after heard no other sound,
Except the rattling of the oak's crisp leaves,　　10
Like the long surf upon a distant shore,
Raking the sea-worn pebbles up and down.
The night had gathered round him: o'er the plain
The city sparkled with its thousand lights,
And sounds of revel fell upon his ear　　15
Harshly and like a curse; above, the sky,
With all its bright sublimity of stars,
Deepened, and on his forehead smote the breeze:
Beauty was all around him and delight,
But from that eve he was alone on earth.　　20

WASHINGTON

James Russell Lowell

Soldier and statesman, rarest unison;
High-poised example of great duties done
Simply as breathing, a world's honors worn
As life's indifferent gifts to all men born;
Dumb for himself, unless it were to God,　　25
But for his barefoot soldiers eloquent,
Tramping the snow to coral where they trod,
Held by his awe in hollow-eyed content;
Modest, yet firm as Nature's self; unblamed
Save by the men his nobler temper shamed;

66   SELECTIONS FOR THE EIGHTH GRADE

Never seduced through show of present good
By other than unsetting lights to steer
New-trimmed in Heaven, nor than his steadfast mood
More steadfast, far from rashness as from fear;
5   Rigid, but with himself first, grasping still
In swerveless poise the wave-beat helm of will;
Not honored then or now because he wooed
The popular voice, but that he still withstood;
Broad-minded, higher-souled, there is but one
10   Who was all this and ours, and all men's, — WASHINGTON.

From *Under the Old Elm*

INCIDENT OF THE FRENCH CAMP

ROBERT BROWNING

NOTE. The storming of Ratisbon took place in May, 1809, during Napoleon's Austrian campaign. It is said that the incident was an actual fact, except that the hero was a man, not a boy.

You know, we French stormed Ratisbon:
    A mile or so away,
On a little mound, Napoleon
    Stood on our storming-day;
15   With neck out-thrust, you fancy how,
    Legs wide, arms locked behind,
As if to balance the prone brow
    Oppressive with its mind.

Just as perhaps he mused "My plans
20   That soar, to earth may fall,
Let once my army-leader Lannes
    Waver at yonder wall," —

INCIDENT OF THE FRENCH CAMP 67

Out 'twixt the battery-smokes there flew
　A rider, bound on bound
Full-galloping; nor bridle drew
　Until he reached the mound.

Then off there flung in smiling joy,
　And held himself erect
By just his horse's mane, a boy:
　You hardly could suspect
(So tight he kept his lips compressed,
　Scarce any blood came through)　　　　　10
You looked twice ere you saw his breast
　Was all but shot in two.

"Well," cried he, "Emperor, by God's grace
　We've got you Ratisbon!
The Marshal's in the marketplace,　　　　15
　And you'll be there anon
To see your flag-bird flap his vans
　Where I, to heart's desire,
Perched him!" The chief's eye flashed; his plans
　Soared up again like fire.　　　　　　20

The chief's eye flashed; but presently
　Softened itself, as sheathes
A film the mother eagle's eye
　When her bruised eaglet breathes;
"You're wounded!" "Nay," the soldier's pride　25
　Touched to the quick, he said:
"I'm killed, Sire!" And his chief beside,
　Smiling the boy fell dead.

SELECTIONS FOR THE EIGHTH GRADE

UNDER THE WILLOWS

JAMES RUSSELL LOWELL

Frank-hearted hostess of the field and wood,
Gypsy, whose roof is every spreading tree,
June is the pearl of our New England year.
Still a surprisal, though expected long,
5 Her coming startles. Long she lies in wait,
Makes many a feint, peeps forth, draws coyly back,
Then, from some southern ambush in the sky,
With one great gush of blossom storms the world.
A week ago the sparrow was divine;
10 The bluebird, shifting his light load of song
From post to post along the cheerless fence,
Was as a rhymer ere the poet come;
But now, O rapture! sunshine winged and voiced,
Pipe blown through by the warm wild breath of the West
15 Shepherding his soft droves of fleecy cloud,
Gladness of woods, skies, waters, all in one,
The bobolink has come, and, like the soul
Of the sweet season vocal in a bird,
Gurgles in ecstasy we know not what
20 Save *June! Dear June! Now God be praised for June.*

May is a pious fraud of the almanac,
A ghastly parody of real Spring
Shaped out of snow and breathed with eastern wind;
Or if, o'er-confident, she trust the date,
25 And, with her handful of anemones,
Herself as shivery, steal into the sun,
The season need but turn his hourglass round,
And Winter suddenly, like crazy Lear,
Reels back, and brings the dead May in his arms,
Her budding breasts and wan dislustered front

UNDER THE WILLOWS

With frosty streaks and drifts of his white beard
All overblown. Then, warmly walled with books,
While my wood fire supplies the sun's defect,
Whispering old forest-sagas in its dreams,
I take my May down from the happy shelf
Where perch the world's rare song-birds in a row,
Waiting my choice to open with full breast,
And beg an alms of springtime, ne'er denied
Indoors by vernal Chaucer, whose fresh woods
Throb thick with merle and mavis all the year.   10

July breathes hot, sallows the crispy fields,
Curls up the wan leaves of the lilac hedge,
And every eve cheats us with show of clouds
That braze the horizon's western rim, or hang
Motionless, with heaped canvas drooping idly,   15
Like a dim fleet by starving men besieged,
Conjectured half, and half descried afar,
Helpless of wind, and seeming to slip back
Adown the smooth curve of the oily sea.

But June is full of invitations sweet,   20
Forth from the chimney's yawn and thrice-read tomes
To leisurely delights and sauntering thoughts
That brook no ceiling narrower than the blue.
The cherry, drest for bridal, at my pane
Brushes, then listens, *Will he come?* The bee,   25
All dusty as a miller, takes his toll
Of powdery gold, and grumbles. What a day
To sun me and do nothing! Nay, I think
Merely to bask and ripen is sometimes
The student's wiser business; the brain   30
That forages all climes to line its cells,
Ranging both worlds on lightest wings of wish,
Will not distill the juices it has sucked

SELECTIONS FOR THE EIGHTH GRADE

To the sweet substance of pellucid thought,
Except for him who hath the secret learned
To mix his blood with sunshine, and to take
The winds into his pulses.   Hush !   'Tis he !
My oriole, my glance of summer fire,
Is come at last, and, ever on the watch,
Twitches the pack-thread I had lightly wound
About the bough to help his housekeeping, —
Twitches and scouts by turns, blessing his luck,
Yet fearing me who laid it in his way,
Nor, more than wiser we in our affairs,
Divines the providence that hides and helps.
Heave, ho!   Heave, ho ! he whistles as the twine
Slackens its hold; *once more, now !* and a flash
Lightens across the sunlight to the elm
Where his mate dangles at her cup of felt.
Nor all his booty is the thread; he trails
My loosened thought with it along the air,
And I must follow, would I ever find
The inward rhyme to all this wealth of life.

APOSTROPHE TO THE OCEAN

Lord Byron

Roll on, thou deep and dark blue ocean, roll !
Ten thousand fleets sweep over thee in vain ;
Man marks the earth with ruin, — his control
Stops with the shore : upon the watery plain,
The wrecks are all thy deed, nor doth remain
A shadow of man's ravage, save his own,
When for a moment, like a drop of rain,
He sinks into thy depths with bubbling groan,
Without a grave, unknell'd, uncoffin'd, and unknown. .

APOSTROPHE TO THE OCEAN

The armaments, which thunderstrike the walls
Of rock-built cities, bidding nations quake,
And monarchs tremble in their capitals;
The oak leviathans, whose huge ribs make
Their clay creator the vain title take
Of lord of thee, and arbiter of war;
These are thy toys, and, as the snowy flake,
They melt into thy yeast of waves, which mar
Alike th' Armada's pride or spoils of Trafalgar.

Thy shores are empires, changed in all save thee: 10
Assyria, Greece, Rome, Carthage, — what are they?
Thy waters wasted them while they were free,
And many a tyrant since; their shores obey
The stranger, slave, or savage; their decay
Has dried up realms to deserts: not so thou;   15
Unchangeable, save to thy wild waves' play,
Time writes no wrinkles on thine azure brow;
Such as creation's dawn beheld, thou rollest now.

Thou glorious mirror, where th' Almighty's form
Glasses itself in tempests; in all time,   20
Calm or convulsed, — in breeze, or gale, or storm,
Icing the pole, or in the torrid clime
Dark heaving; — boundless, endless, and sublime,
The image of Eternity, — the throne
Of the Invisible: even from out thy slime   25
The monsters of the deep are made: each zone
Obeys thee: thou goest forth, dread, fathomless, alone.

And I have loved thee, Ocean! and my joy
Of youthful sports was on thy breast to be
Borne, like thy bubbles, onward; from a boy   30
I wanton'd with thy breakers, — they to me
Were a delight; and, if the freshening sea

SELECTIONS FOR THE EIGHTH GRADE

Made them a terror, 'twas a pleasing fear;
For I was, as it were, a child of thee,
And trusted to thy billows far and near,
And laid my hand upon thy mane, — as I do here.

TO A SKYLARK

PERCY BYSSHE SHELLEY

Hail to thee, blithe Spirit ! —
Bird thou never wert —
That from Heaven, or near it,
Pourest thy full heart
In profuse strains of unpremeditated art.

10   Higher still and higher
From the earth thou springest
Like a cloud of fire;
The blue deep thou wingest,
And singing still dost soar, and soaring ever singest.

15   In the golden lightning
Of the sunken sun,
O'er which clouds are brightening,
Thou dost float and run,
Like an unbodied joy whose race is just begun.

20   The pale purple even
Melts around thy flight;
Like a star of heaven
In the broad daylight
Thou art unseen, but yet I hear thy shrill delight,

TO A SKYLARK

73

Keen as are the arrows
Of that silver sphere,
Whose intense lamp narrows
In the white dawn clear,
Until we hardly see, we feel that it is there.

All the earth and air
With thy voice is loud,
As, when night is bare,
From one lonely cloud
The moon rains out her beams, and heaven is overflowed.　　10

What thou art we know not;
What is most like thee?
From rainbow clouds there flow not
Drops so bright to see,
As from thy presence showers a rain of melody.　　15

Like a poet hidden
In the light of thought,
Singing hymns unbidden,
Till the world is wrought
To sympathy with hopes and fears it heeded not;　　20

Like a high-born maiden,
In a palace tower,
Soothing her love-laden
Soul in secret hour
With music sweet as love, which overflows her bower;　　25

Like a glowworm golden,
In a dell of dew,
Scattering unbeholden
Its aerial hue
Among the flowers and grass which screen it from the view;

74 SELECTIONS FOR THE EIGHTH GRADE

Like a rose embowered
  In its own green leaves,
By warm winds deflowered,
  Till the scent it gives
5 Makes faint with too much sweet these heavy-wingèd thieves.

Sound of vernal showers
  On the twinkling grass,
Rain-awakened flowers,
  All that ever was
10 Joyous, and clear, and fresh, thy music doth surpass.

Teach us, sprite or bird,
  What sweet thoughts are thine:
I have never heard
  Praise of love or wine
15 That panted forth a flood of rapture so divine.

Chorus hymeneal,
  Or triumphal chant,
Matched with thine would be all
  But an empty vaunt
20 A thing wherein we feel there is some hidden want.

What objects are the fountains
  Of thy happy strain?
What fields, or waves, or mountains?
  What shapes of sky or plain?
25 What love of thine own kind? what ignorance of pain?

With thy clear, keen joyance
  Languor cannot be;
Shadow of annoyance
  Never came near thee;
Thou lovest, but ne'er knew love's sad satiety.

TO A SKYLARK   75

Waking or asleep,
 Thou of death must deem
Things more true and deep
 Than we mortals dream;
Or how could thy notes flow in such a crystal stream?   5

We look before and after,
 And pine for what is not;
Our sincerest laughter
 With some pain is fraught;
Our sweetest songs are those that tell of saddest thought.   10

Yet if we could scorn
 Hate, and pride, and fear;
If we were things born
 Not to shed a tear,
I know not how thy joy we ever should come near.   15

Better than all measures
 Of delightful sound,
Better than all treasures
 That in books are found,
Thy skill to poet were, thou scorner of the ground!   20

Teach me half the gladness
 That thy brain must know,
Such harmonious madness
 From my lips would flow,
The world should listen then, as I am listening now.   25

NOTES

(The figures in heavy-faced type refer to pages, the figures in lighter type to lines.)

THE MAN WITHOUT A COUNTRY

[Frederic Ingham, the " I " of the story, is supposed to be a retired naval officer.]

2 21 *esprit de corps* (ĕs prē' dę kôr') the loyal pride and energy of a united company of people.

2 27 **Ross** : a British general who captured Washington in 1814 and burned the public buildings.

2 34 *non mi ricordo* (nŏn mē rē kôr'dō) : " I do not remember."

4 7 **to break on the wheel** : literally, to torture and kill by cruel means ; figuratively, to dispose of effectually.

4 8 **Clarences of the then House of York** : the duke of Clarence was executed for treason in 1473. He had been a double traitor, first to the House of York, the governing power of England, and later to the House of Lancaster.

9 13 **Paraguay** : a name once given to an immense region in South America.

9 18 **Hesiod** : an epic poet of Greece who lived several centuries before the Christian Era.

9 19 **Canning** : George Canning, a famous English statesman.

11 13 **braggadocio** : empty boasting ; bravado. The word comes from the name of a vain fellow in Spenser's poem, " The Faerie Queen."

11 25 **Fléchier** : an eloquent French preacher of the seventeenth century.

12 19 **so much room** : the ladies of 1863 wore huge hoop skirts.

12 28 **Lady Hamilton** : a famous English beauty.

12 34 *contretemps* (kŏn'tr tŏN) : an embarrassing accident or situation.

13 2 **contra-dances** : a corruption of " country-dances." In these the dancers are ranged in two opposite lines.

13 31 **tongues and sounds** : a play upon words. The tongues and sounds (air bladders or rudimentary lungs) of codfish are often sold together by New England fishermen ; this used to be a common street cry in Gloucester and Marblehead.

14 13 **the Iron Mask** : a mysterious prisoner who always wore a mask, and who was confined in French prisons for twenty-five years. No one has

77

78 SELECTIONS FOR THE EIGHTH GRADE

ever succeeded in establishing his identity, but it is commonly supposed that he was an Italian, named Matthioli, who had tried to injure Louis XIV. The mask was of black velvet, not iron, and even at the death of its wearer, in 1703, it was not removed from his face.

14 15 Junius: the unknown author of a series of famous letters which appeared in an English newspaper between 1769 and 1772. These letters attacked many of the public characters of the day, even royalty itself. It is now believed that they were written by Sir Philip Francis.

16 1 Nukahiwa Islands: these belong to the Marquesas group in the South Pacific.

17 30 Middle Passage: the middle or sea passage in the long journey of African slaves from their homes to the American slave market.

18 31 Beledeljereed: "the country of dates," a name formerly given to a portion of the Barbary States. This region has had for many years a large number of French residents.

19 6 Kroomen: members of a Liberian tribe of negroes, noted for their skill as boatmen.

19 7 Fernando Po: an island in the Gulf of Guinea on the west coast of Africa.

19 18 *deus ex machina* (dē'ŭs ĕx măk'ĭ na): a person suddenly introduced to untangle a difficulty, in allusion to the custom in the old Greek tragedies of bringing in a god by stage machinery to solve hopeless problems.

19 20 Cape Palmas: a headland of Liberia.

20 5 barracoon: a temporary barrack or shelter for slaves.

21 23 St. Thomas harbor: the island of St. Thomas, which has a fine harbor, is in the West Indies.

22 1 *ben trovato* (bĕn trō vä'tō): well invented.

23 28 Tamaulipas: a state of Mexico, bounded on the north by Texas.

24 4 Captain Back: an English navigator. Sir Thomas Roe was an English ambassador in the time of James I.

28 5 Benjamin Lincoln: General Lincoln received Cornwallis's sword at the surrender of Yorktown. It is an interesting coincidence, in view of Philip Nolan's question, that the ancestors of both Benjamin Lincoln and Abraham Lincoln came from the same county in England and settled in Hingham, Massachusetts. Early in the eighteenth century the great-great-grandfather of President Lincoln moved to New Jersey.

THE SKELETON IN ARMOR

[There is probably little foundation for the claim that the Norsemen built the stone tower at Newport.]

30 19 skald (skäld): a Norse reciter of heroic poems.

NOTES

30 20 **saga** (sä′gä) : an ancient Norse legend.

31 4 **gerfalcon** (jĕr′fak′n) : a large species of falcon.

31 14 **werewolf** : in folklore, a person who has assumed the form of a wolf.

31 25 **wassail bout** : a drinking contest.

31 29 **Berserk** : a wild and savage warrior.

33 22 **skaw** : headland.

35 7 **Skoal** : a salutation used in drinking a health ; equivalent to *Hail !*

HORATIUS

[The Tarquinian dynasty had been banished from Rome, and a republic had been established under two magistrates called consuls. Tarquin, after a vain effort to recover his throne, gained the alliance of Porsena, ruler of Etruria.]

The year of the city CCCLX : 394 B.C.

Livy, Polybius, and **Dionysius** were Latin historians.

35 9 **Lars** : a title of honor.

35 9 **Clusium** : an important city.

36 14 **amain** : see note on page 49, line 25.

36 21 **Volaterræ** : the modern Volterra.

36 22 **the far-famed hold** : a strong natural fortress. Volterra stands on a lofty rock.

36 25 **Populonia** : a town in Etruria.

37 1 **Pisæ** : a town on the site of modern Pisa.

37 3 **Massilia** : modern Marseilles ; settled by the Greeks, and an important city even in early times.

37 3 **triremes** : warships with three banks of oars.

37 5 **Clanis** : a tributary of the Tiber.

37 7 **Cortona** : a town in Etruria or Tuscany.

37 13 **Clitummus** : a little river in Italy.

37 16 **Volsinian mere** : a lake in Etruria ; it is now called Bolsena.

37 22 **the milk-white steer** : belonging to a famous breed of oxen used for sacrifice on great occasions.

37 25 **Arretium** : the modern Arezzo, a Tuscan province.

37 27 **Umbro** : a river of Etruria.

38 1 **vats of Luna** : the wine vats in the town of Luna, where the juice was trodden out of the grapes.

38 2 **must** : the juice of the grapes.

38 5 **thirty chosen prophets** : the augurs, who foretold events and interpreted the will of the gods.

38 10 **the verses** : written prophecies.

80 SELECTIONS FOR THE EIGHTH GRADE

38 11 **traced from the right**: written from right to left as in Hebrew or Arabic.

38 19 **Nurscia**: a goddess of the Volsinians, probably the Roman Fortuna.

38 22 **tale**: number. Cf. *tally*.

39 7 **the Tusculan Mamilius**: a son-in-law of Tarquin the Proud, belonging to Tusculum, a town of Latium.

39 11 **champaign**: open fields and plains. In English verse the word is accented on the first syllable,

40 5 **the rock Tarpeian**: a precipice overlooking the Tiber. Here, in later times, traitors were hurled to their death.

40 9 **Fathers**: senators. We have kept the expression " city fathers " for the city authorities.

40 17 **Verbenna**: a name of Macaulay's own invention.

40 17 **Ostia**: the port of Rome.

40 19 **Astur**: another invention of the poet's.

40 19 **Janiculum**: a high hill west of the Tiber; not one of the " seven hills " on which the city was built.

40 21 **I wis**: originally ywis, meaning *certainly*.

41 6 **straight**: straightway; immediately.

42 7 **Umbrian**: Umbria was in eastern and central Italy.

42 8 **Gaul**: this refers to the people of northern Italy, or " cisalpine Gaul."

42 11 **port and vest**: manner and dress.

42 12 **Lucumo**: the title of an Etruscan prince.

42 15 **fourfold shield**: made of four layers of hide or metal.

42 16 **brand**: sword. This use of the word will be found to be very common in Scott's poems.

42 19 **Thrasymene**: Lake Thrasymenus.

42 26 **false Sextus**: a son of Tarquin the Proud. His wickedness and cruel treachery had made him hateful to the people of Rome.

43 17 **Horatius**: surnamed Cocles; he was a patrician, since he belonged to one of the three original tribes.

44 1 **the holy maidens**: six maidens, known as the vestal virgins, whose duty it was to keep the fire burning on the altar of Vesta, the goddess of the fireside.

44 9 **strait**: narrow, not *straight*.

44 14 **Ramnian**: belonging to another of the three tribes. Herminius represented the third.

45 11 **Tribunes**: officers of the city chosen from among the plebeians to protect the plebeians' interests.

45 18 **harness**: armor.

45 21 **Commons**: the plebeians; the common people.

NOTES

46 22 **Ilva** : Elba.

46 28 **the pale waves** : the waters of the Nar were remarkable for their sulphurous quality and white appearance.

47 9 **Falerii** : a town in Etruria.

47 12 **the rover of the sea** : there were many pirates as well as merchants among the Etruscans.

47 16 **Cosa** : a town in Etruria.

47 18 **Albinia** : a river of Etruria.

47 27 **Campania** : a seacoast country southeast of Latium. Study an ancient map to get a clear idea of all the above-mentioned district.

47 27 **hinds** : peasants or farm servants.

48 21 **the she-wolf's litter** : refers to the tradition that the founders of Rome — Romulus and Remus — were suckled by a wolf.

49 17 **Mount Alvernus** : a mountain in northern Etruria.

49 21 **the pale augurs** : the augurs carefully watched and interpreted the effects of lightning.

49 25 **amain** : with all his force. We still say " with might and *main.*" *Amain* sometimes means *without ceasing.* Cf. p. 36, l. 14.

52 23 **constant** : steadfast ; unwavering.

52 29 **grace** : mercy.

53 5 **Palatinus** : the hill on which the homes of the patricians stood.

53 9 **father Tiber** : the early Romans looked upon all objects in nature as possessing each an invisible spirit. The river-god was supposed to dwell in the Tiber.

53 23 **crest** : the helmet, or the plume worn upon the helmet.

54 16 **Bare bravely up his chin** : in a footnote to this line Macaulay quotes from Scott

> Our ladye bare upp her chinne.
> > *Ballad of Childe Waters*

> Never heavier man and horse
> Stemmed a midnight torrent's force ;
>
> . . . .
>
> Yet, through good heart and our Lady's grace,
> At length he gained the landing place.
> > *Lay of the Last Minstrel*, I.

54 21 **Heaven help him** : compare Porsena's generous praise with the attitude of Sextus.

55 5 **corn-land** : lands belonging to the state. They were generally acquired in war.

55 8 **could plow** : *i.e. could plow around.*

55 13 **Comitium** : an open space adjoining the forum.

82 SELECTIONS FOR THE EIGHTH GRADE

55 24 **Volscian**: the Volscians were dangerous enemies in the early days of the Republic.

55 25 **Juno**: the wife of Jupiter, the chief of the gods. Juno was the protectress of women.

56 7 **Algidus**: a mountain of Latium.

THE SINGING LEAVES

[Among the earliest forms of poetry is the ballad. It was originally a story in rhythmical form which was recited or sung, often with some instrumental accompaniment. For generations the old British ballads were handed down from one singer to another without taking written shape. When at last these old songs were printed, they contained many rough and uneven lines, but they had a charm which gives them a place among our chief literary treasures. Lowell imitated the ballad meter very successfully. In reading the verses the lilt and swing of the music should be kept in mind rather than strict rules of accentuation.]

57 1 **fairings**: presents; originally, as here, those brought from a fair.

57 3 **Vanity Fair**: a fair for the sale of trifles and luxuries, described in Bunyan's " Pilgrim's Progress."

57 3 **boun**: bound.

57 20 **the Singing Leaves**: taken from a story in the " Arabian Nights."

60 18 **but and**: and also.

RHŒCUS

61 3 **the master key**: a key so made as to open different locks.

61 13 **the hazel twig**: it is a matter of widespread belief that a forked twig, preferably of witch hazel, if held by a person sensitive to certain mysterious influences, will bend toward the ground to indicate hidden springs of water. Science places no faith in this " divining rod."

61 30 **Attic**: belonging to Attica, or its principal city, Athens.

63 6 **idle shepherd's pipe**: shepherds were wont to amuse themselves with a simple musical instrument, consisting of a tube of reed or wood.

64 24 **or by day or night**: either by day or night.

INCIDENT OF THE FRENCH CAMP

66 11 **Ratisbon**: an important town in Bavaria on the Danube river.

66 15 **you fancy how**: a well-known picture of Napoleon, painted by Haydon, represents him in this attitude.

66 17 **prone**: literally, *sloping downward*.

67 17 **vans**: wings.

NOTES

83

UNDER THE WILLOWS

[The selection given is the prelude to a long poem.]

68 28 **like crazy Lear** : see " King Lear," Act V, scene iii, lines 256–257.

69 10 **merle and mavis** : the European blackbird and song thrush.

69 14 **braze** : to cover with brass.

71 9 **the Armada** : a great Spanish fleet sent against England by Philip II. It was dispersed and partly destroyed by English ships and by terrible storms.

71 9 **Trafalgar** : Cape Trafalgar'; this is a headland on the southwestern coast of Spain, where in 1805 a naval battle took place between the English ships under Lord Nelson, and the combined French and Spanish fleets. Lord Nelson was mortally wounded, but the English were victorious. It was in this battle that Nelson's famous signal was given, " England expects every man to do his duty." Trafalgar Square, in London, where the Nelson monument stands, is usually called Trå fål' gar Square.

PRONOUNCING VOCABULARY OF
PROPER NAMES

Ăl bĭn'Ĭ a
Al'ġĭ dŭs
Ăl vĕr'nŭs
Ăp'ĕn nīne
Ä rez'zo
 (rĕt sō)
Ăr rē'ti um
 (shum)
Ā'rŭnṣ
Ăs'tûr
Au'nŭs
Au'sûr

Băb'ĭng tọn
Beau'rĕ gärd
 (ō)
Bĕl'ĕd ĕl jĕr ēēd'
Bĕr'sĕrk
Bou lō*gne*'
 (ɴ)
Bue'nōs *A*ī'res
 (ă)   (ă)
Bysshe (bĭsh)

Caĭ'rō
Căm pā'nĭ a
Çĭl'nĭ ŭs
Çĭ mĭn'Ĭ an
Clā'nĭs
Clĭ tŭm'nŭs

Clū'si um
 (zhŭm)
Cō'clēṣ
Cŏ mĭ'ti um
 (shŭm)
Côr tō'nạ
Cō'ṣạ
Crŭs tŭ mē'rĭ ŭm

Dĭ ŏ nў'si us
 (shŭs)

Ė trụ'rĭ ạ
Ė trŭs'can

Fă lē'rĭ ĭ
Fĕr năn'dō Pō
Fléchier (flă shĭ ā)
Fôr tū'na

Grēēn'ō*ugh*

Hĕr mĭn'Ĭ ŭs
Hĕ'si od
 (shọd)
Hŏn dụ'räs
Hŏ rā'ti us
 (shŭs)

Ĭl'vạ
Ing'hạɪn
Ĭn trĕp'Ĭd

Jă nĭc'ŭ lŭm
Jūn'ius
 (yŭs)
Jū'nō

Là*nn*es
Lärṣ
Lär'ti us
 (shŭs)
Lā'ti an
 (shạn)
Lau'sŭ lŭs
Lei ces'tĕr
 (lĕs)
Lĕp Ĭ dŏp'tĕr a
Lĕ vănt'
Lĭn'na*è* ŭs
Lĭv'ў
Lū'cŭ mō
Lū'nạ

Mà cau'laў
Mă mĭl'Ĭ ŭs
Mär que'sạs
 (kā)
Măs'sac
Măs sĭl'Ĭ a
Măt *th*ï ō'lĭ

Năr
Nĕ quĭ'nŭm

86 · SELECTIONS FOR THE EIGHTH GRADE

Nụ kä hĭ'wa (vạ)

Nûr'sci ạ
(shĭ)

Ŏc'nŭs

Ôr'lĕ ạng

Os'ti a
(tyä)

Păl ä tĭ'nŭs

Păl'mäs

Păr'ạ guäy

Pĭ'cŭs

Pĭ'ṣaē

Pŏ lўb'ĭ ŭs

Pŏp ụ lŏ'nĭ ạ

Pôr'sẹ nạ

Răm'nĭ ạn

Răt'ĭs bŏn

Rhoē'cŭs

Rĭ'ō Ja nei'rō
(zhạ) (ä)

Rŏm'ụ lŭs

Sär dĭn'ĭ ạ

Sẽ'i us
(yŭs)

Sĕx'tŭs

Spū'rĭ ŭs

Sū'trĭ ŭm

Tä mä ụ lĭ'päs

Tär pē'ian
(yạn)

Tär'quĭn

Tăt'nạll

Thĕs'sạ lў

Thräs'ў mēne

Tĭ'bĕr

Tĭ fẽr'nŭm

Tĭ'ti an
(shạn)

Tŏ lŭm'nĭ ŭs

Tŭs'cŭ lạn

Tŭs'cŭ lŭm

Ŭm'brĭ an

Ŭm'brō

Ûr'gō

Vallandigham
(vạ lăn'dẹ găm)

Vaughan

Ve'rä Cruz
(ä)   (oos)

Vĕr bĕn'nạ

Vĕs'ta

Vĭ'kĭng

Vŏl a tĕr'raē

Vŏl'sci an
(shan)

Vŏl sĭn'ĭ an

Vŏl sĭn'ĭ ŭm

Wät'roŭs

Zụ'lụ

CPSIA information can be obtained
at www.ICGtesting.com
Printed in the USA
LVOW04s0254061115
461381LV00016B/218/P